"*Lifestyle Lawyer* is an excellent resource to help women attorneys navigate the ever-changing (and yet at times, rather stagnant) legal industry. The practical advice coupled with real life stories make this a useful guidebook for women at all stages of their career. As one of the early pioneers of 'new law,' I truly wish I had something like this to help me along the way."

Nicole Nehama Auerbach is a founder of Valorem Law Group, a firm nationally recognized for blazing the Alternative Fee Arrangement trail, and is a founder of ElevateNext Law, the only law firm in the U.S. backed by a global legal service provider, Elevate Services, to provide end to end solutions to customers.

"While you should have chosen business school instead of law school (just sayin'), you should totally check out this book. Holcomb's insights will help you broaden the way you think about your career trajectory in the ever-shifting sands of the legal industry. Because if you're going to be a lawyer, you might as well be a good one."

Paul Ollinger, Nationally-touring comedian, Dartmouth MBA, and author, You Should Totally Get an MBA

"An inspiring and encouraging book for every lawyer asking 'How can I be a successful lawyer and still have a life?' Ms. Holcomb's book is a must read for all lawyers navigating the tremendous changes in the legal industry while trying to find the best path to being a 'unique, happy and successful lifestyle attorney.' "

Karen G. Crutchfield, Member, Wimberly Lawson Wright Daves & Jones, PLLC

"Lee Holcomb's book, *Lifestyle Lawyer*, empowers women lawyers to forge career paths that fit their lives. Holcomb dispels the myth that the only options are to sacrifice everything to become a partner in a law firm or to quit. She explains how women lawyers can build careers that let them use their unique talents to make a meaningful difference, while also having time for family and personal pursuits. Holcomb discusses the opportunities and challenges facing female lawyers and outlines in great detail different career paths. *Lifestyle Lawyer* helps women take control of their careers to create happy, fulfilling lives."

Beth Cabrera–Senior Scholar, Center for the Advancement of Well-Being at George Mason University and Author of Beyond Happy: Women, Work, and Well-Being

"Lifestyle lawyer is more than just an inspiring, rationalized view on the complex world of the legal profession. It is also the insight of a woman sharing with her readers a way to unbundle the intertwined connections of wishes, aspirations, with the unexpected that life brings in."

Aysha Jessica Beavers–Ph.D. candidate at Zhongnan University of Economics and Law

"Right out of law school I went to work with a large and prestigious law firm. Had three children then moved overseas to Warsaw, Poland with my husband for his job. I have no regrets for taking the eight years to raise my children. Getting back to law after eight years out, however, was not easy. So I moved on. I was lucky to get a Director level non-legal job (my legal background helped) with a global organization. Holcomb's advice in *Lifestyle Lawyer* is on point, valuable and insightful. In the after-life of lawyering, take control of your next career and make it one that interests you and works with your lifestyle. *Lifestyle Lawyer* will help you make your next career fit into your life rather than the other way around."

Francesca Laursen, Director Multilateral Relations & the Green Climate Fund at the World Wildlife Fund

"This book is a must read for any woman looking to reassess the path of her legal career."

Holly Renken, Attorney, Office of Judge Kenny Armstrong, Tennessee Court of Appeals

LIFESTYLE
LAWYER

LEE HOLCOMB

LIFESTYLE LAWYER

THE FEMALE ATTORNEY'S GUIDE TO DESIGNING A LAW CAREER YOU LOVE

LEE HOLCOMB

Lifestyle Lawyer: The Female Attorney's Guide to
Designing a Law Career You Love

By Lee Holcomb

1. Self-Help/General 2. Body, Mind & Spirit/General 3. Law/General

ISBN: 978-1-935953-98-2 Paperback
ISBN: 978-1-935953-99-9 EBook
Library of Congress Control Number: 2018949491

Cover design by Lewis Argell

Printed in the United States of America

Authority Publishing
11230 Gold Express Dr. #310-413
Gold River, CA 95670
800-877-1097
www.AuthorityPublishing.com

To Jackson & Vincent—your presence brings so much happiness and joy to my life. May you pass through each stage of life with clarity, enrichment and just a little against the grain.

To Mary Valentine—Thank you for always encouraging me and supporting me in my dreams.

In loving memory of Ms. Holcomb July 1911 – October 15, 1994

"Change is the core of growth. Recognizing that every career change, every professional and personal role I have played in my life, has enriched and informed the next path, has allowed me not to fear change, but to embrace it. I observe the fluidity in which clay can be transformed, each of its stages needs to happen in order for the next to work. Like clay, we need to allow change in order to be transformed into new shapes bringing past experiences and accumulated knowledge with us."

—*Dubhe Carreno*[1]

TABLE OF CONTENTS

Chapter 5: Define What You Do Best in Your Life and Work 48

Chapter 6: Distinguish Yourself in Your Job and Your Life 59

Chapter 7: Network and Establish Yourself as an Expert. 71

INTRODUCTION

I started my career at a traditional law firm. If you'd asked me then, I would have told you emphatically that I loved it and would stay with Leitner, Williams, Dooley & Napolitan until I retired. But life changes, and we sometimes have to make difficult choices. For me, this meant leaving the firm in 2006, just one year after becoming a partner.

Why would I do this? Like many women, my hard work led to a certain level of professional success—right when I wanted to expand my family. I wanted a second child—and I wanted more time with my kids than being a partner at a firm would allow. Not to mention that my husband was eyeing a position with the U.S. State Department. So on December 23, 2006, with a three-year-old and a six-month-old in tow, I boarded a plane from Knoxville, Tennessee, and moved to Warsaw, Poland, intending to take time off from practicing law. I knew it was the right decision.

But knowing something is right doesn't make it easy. It may not surprise you that just months after leaving my job, I was already looking to get back to work. I missed my career, but I needed a job that would allow me to also have time with my family.

Shortly after we arrived in Warsaw, I started teaching yoga at the U.S. Embassy. I also began planning my return to the legal workforce. My husband's second assignment took us to Chennai, India. Six months later I took a part-time position with Cobra Legal Solutions, an international legal process outsourcing (LPO) company that provides legal support services to large U.S.–based companies and law firms. Thus began my second legal career path, which would eventually lead me to become COO and Director of Legal Solutions at Cobra.

Making the decision to move overseas and ultimately take a position with a young company in a start-up industry ended up being one of the best decisions of my life. My time at Cobra brought me many great experiences and lessons that are an integral part of who I am today, as a person and an attorney. If I had stuck to a traditional and expected career path as a partner in a law firm I would never have had this incredible experience.

I also feel fortunate that I was able to *stay in* the workforce while I was living overseas. It is important for new female lawyers to realize the advantages of staying in the workforce, even when they are getting married, having children or taking care of an aging parent. Not only does it provide financial security, it also prepares you to handle the unexpected that life may bring—death, divorce, unexpected financial changes, or even a renewed interest in having a career at a later age in life. This doesn't mean you have to keep your 60+-hour-a-week job at the law firm. There will be times in your life where different jobs make more sense for you because they provide the flexibility to work from home, work part-time or are less stressful. You've worked hard to get where you are. Utilize the new legal jobs on the market to stay in the workforce.

As I finish writing *Lifestyle Lawyer*, I'm embarking on my third legal career: as an independent contractor and business owner. I'm also in the fourth year of operating a small pottery company—this venture keeps me grounded and connected to my artistic side. As in the past, I question myself as I go about the process of making this career change. But life has taught me that some of the most important elements in navigating change are patience, presence and persistence—along with taking time to reflect on how I've changed and what I want and need at this time in my life.

Multiple factors have led me to this decision. In our changing legal landscape, I see so many opportunities on the horizon for lawyers to do things differently, and I'm excited to continue to be a part of this legal revolution. I've also always dreamed about starting my own business. I'd hit a point in my prior position where it just wasn't working for me anymore. When you realize that your work is no longer bringing you happiness, growth and fulfillment, it's time to make a change. In my case, I was feeling a level of stress, confusion and unhappiness that was affecting my performance at work and my relationships outside of work. I knew it was time to go.

Although it may sound like this process was simple, I can assure you it has been filled with difficult moments, a few tears and hard choices—and to be honest, I don't expect that to change. Life and work are challenging, and that's part of what makes them rewarding, fulfilling and continually interesting. Recognizing that I needed a change and reflecting on my prior experiences eventually allowed me to take the next step in my career path without fear. I was comfortable knowing that I was embarking on a new and enriching life experience.

My prior careers have taught me how to look at things differently: I want to share this knowledge with you. Leaving my job and setting out on a new legal path at this point in my life was a hard decision. In fact, I first started developing this book as a guide and resource to help me grapple with many tough career and life decisions.

But making this change has already allowed me to grow as a person and a leader, and to help others in a similar situation. It's also been a *fun* process. Along with writing this book and starting a new business, I've taken on new goals, challenges and rewarding responsibilities. I tell you this because I want you to know two things: first, you're not alone. You have plenty of good company—many other experienced and successful attorneys have questioned their career paths. Second, if you're early on in your career you may be pondering where you're headed. The process of questioning, change and growth is a natural part of life—embrace and enjoy it!

When you complete this process, you'll be on the right path for you, just as I found I'm on the right path for my family and me. How will you get there? Don't discount your experiences:

they're important, they're a part of you! It's only when you identify with your unique self that you find your voice and can help
yourself and others. You can absolutely revitalize your life and
your career—you just need a plan and some dedication. But you
also need to realize that nothing is set in stone: even the perfect
career plan can throw you an unexpected opportunity or an
equally unexpected curve ball. Be prepared to look at your life
as full of possibilities—educate yourself with new skills so you'll
be ready for them.

Lawyers who are prepared to take chances and be flexible with
their careers and expectations will find many new options in the
new legal industry. Technology is here to stay. Reading this book,
evaluating the shifts taking place in our profession, and determining how you'll fit into the changing industry are important
first steps in revitalizing your legal career. Redesigning your law
career to fit your life and the changing profession might happen
quickly, depending on the path you choose, but most likely it
won't happen overnight. To arrive at your new destination, you'll
need perseverance to keep moving forward, however slowly, until
you arrive in the life and career you want.

Do you want to be a "lifestyle lawyer" or have a job with
"lifestyle benefits?"

A lifestyle lawyer is a term I've coined to describe attorneys
who value their law degrees, but have figured out which part of
the practice works for them and how to incorporate it into their
lives. They're not necessarily tied to the traditional role of the
attorney. In many instances, a lifestyle lawyer's legal practice will
be extremely specialized, making her a subject-matter expert in a
particular area. In other instances, a lifestyle lawyer will be more
involved in the business side of the company, but her expertise
will still be a component of what she does on a daily basis. A
lifestyle lawyer may also be an attorney who has figured out that
they want to spend more time at home and are willing to take
less pay if they can work remotely. In all instances, a lifestyle
lawyer is a creative personality who has interests outside of the
legal profession and is looking for a new way to live and work.

LIFESTYLE TIP – *You're already a female lifestyle lawyer if: you're a female, you're a lawyer, you're passionate about your job and you have interests aside from the law.*

So the question is, who are you and what do you want?

To determine this, you'll first need to look inward, reflecting on where you are, who you are, and what you value. You can then use this clarified awareness to identify a vision for your life. When you know what you want and where you want to go, you'll need to first set goals that take you there, then learn how to support your efforts to reach those goals. The first half of the book (Section 1) will support you in this essential work.

In the second half (Section 2), we'll shift gears to look at six different career paths and how they're being affected by the evolving legal market. These paths include: the law firm path, the corporate path, the solo practitioner and legal consultant path, the alternative legal service provider path, the eDiscovery path, and the cybersecurity and privacy path. For each path, we will look at the impact of technology, financial implications, and the stories of successful female lawyers who've taken that path.

My hope for this book is that it helps you determine and shape a career perfectly tailored to you—your strengths, your vision, your inner wisdom—and provides detailed information that helps you see available opportunities and claim your happiness.

With these intentions, let's get to work!

SECTION 1

YOUR CAREER PATH AS A FEMALE LIFESTYLE ATTORNEY

1

WHERE ARE YOU ON YOUR LAWYER PATH?

I have a secret to share. I didn't go to law school because I wanted to be a lawyer; I went to law school because I was an artist.

Early in my art career, I was working with a store designing and selling floor clothes (custom-made rugs that I designed and painted). As the relationship progressed, the store owner and I decided to enter into a more formal relationship involving a joint business venture, so we could take my artwork to Mexico and have it replicated and mass produced.

Enter the contracts and lawyers!

The process quickly became overwhelming and a little scary. As a 22-year-old with no experience of business and legal documents, I didn't know how to handle the contracts placed in front of me, and I didn't have the resources to hire an attorney to help. So I walked away.

I wasn't giving up forever. I still wanted to create, build and design things. But I also wanted to be able to market and sell the things I made, and I had just learned how complicated that could become. Before returning to the art world, I wanted to better equip myself to deal with the business side of being an artist. Not to mention that it couldn't hurt to have a more reliable way to support myself. I figured a law degree would give me the leg up I needed. It may not make sense to everyone—but that's why I went.

It was clear from day one of law school that I was in the minority. Many of my fellow students had a strong desire to practice law; they had taken pre-law classes in college, or at the very least had one or more parents who were attorneys. Most also had a better understanding than I did of what our professors expected of us. I was definitely starting a little behind the curve, but I soon started to get the hang of things. In fact, as I studied and then later began practicing law, I discovered that many of the same skills used to make great art also drive a successful law practice. Think creativity, attention to detail and focus.

And while I may have been in the minority when I entered law school to support an art career, I've met more artist-lawyers during my 20 years in practice than you might expect. I've increasingly run across lawyers in art classes—some who have even given up on law and are making art full-time. In several instances, I knew them as artists for months or years before I knew they were attorneys too. And when you consider the number of lawyers-turned-artists in the public eye, like the popular authors John Grisham, Eric Garner and Scott Turow, and the celebrated visual artists Henri Matisse and Wassily Kandinsky, the connection between law and art is even more pronounced.

Is creating art simply therapy for the stressed-out lawyer? Or is it that the lawyer is more creative and artistic than people think? Creating art can certainly be therapeutic after a long stressful day at work, but there's more to it than that: creativity comes naturally to many lawyers. Creating art isn't that different from conceiving a brilliant legal argument or defense. Both require a unique perspective, frequent tweaking and rethinking, and courage in execution.

I would argue that attorneys, like artists, need the freedom to exercise their creativity in order to thrive and have a balanced, healthy life. Yet most attorneys aren't being encouraged or allowed to tap into their creative talents. Years ago, lawyers could be mavericks, developing ideas and solving problems on their own in each unique case, but today's legal industry has become tethered by procedure, regulations and tradition. I wonder if this is one reason why the legal profession has a higher-than-average problem with substance abuse, stress and depression.

I'm hopeful that this will take a turn for the better as technology continues to advance. Technology could be the door opener that allows attorneys to change the legal landscape and create new, more fulfilling ways to practice law in the 21st century. Instead of death by robots, technology may instead bring a renaissance in legal practice that once more melds both art and science.

For me, creativity has always been a part of my life: both as an attorney and my life outside the office. After all, it's what brought me into a legal office in the first place! Until I started writing this book, though, I'd never told anyone the real reason I went to law school. The point of sharing my story now is to show you that we all don't need to take the same journey. My experiences and reflection while writing this book have taught me that one of my job requirements is creativity. It trumps money. I need to be in a position where I'm providing creative input and helping to build a product, a service and relationships.

What I'm talking about here is best captured by the title of this book: *Lifestyle Lawyer*. I've coined this term to identify attorneys who value their law degrees, but have figured out how to make their legal careers inspiring and meaningful and how to incorporate those careers into their lives as a whole.

And being a lifestyle lawyer means that you get *lifestyle benefits*. I don't mean just traditional fringe benefits like 401(k) plans or extra vacation weeks. What I mean by lifestyle benefits are the unique attributes of a particular job that let you be a whole person at work and engage your own interests and skills: things like writing, public speaking, artistic expression, networking, and engagement in business development, along with the more traditional benefits such as the ability to work remotely, work part-time, or make more money. Obviously, what one lifestyle attorney considers a lifestyle benefit will not necessarily be one to another. But, the end result should allow you to be more successful and happy at work and home.

I hope that through reading my story—and those of other female attorneys—you can fully appreciate your own distinct journey as a lawyer. I hope you learn that your path doesn't need to look a certain way: there's no set image or position you have to achieve. What you *do* need, in order to feel good and be happy, is a vision that gives your life meaning. When you identify your necessary lifestyle benefits, your vision and your strengths, and begin to orient your career around these, you'll become happier and more positive, and your life will start to flow. You'll be on your own right path.

> LIFESTYLE TIP – *Lifestyle lawyers have identified the skills, the hobbies, the activities, and the people they enjoy; they make time—either at work or outside of it—to continue their craft. These are the lifestyle benefits of life that will make you happy and inspire others to do the same. This is our goal: to help you identify and incorporate what's most important to you into your life and career. Although I'm not creating art as my primary occupation, I did start making pottery in 2015—I love the whole process of creating and selling my work. It is a lifestyle benefit that I want to cultivate in my life.*

HOW TO GET ON THE RIGHT PATH

I'm convinced that a successful legal career can be fulfilling and meaningful. But that doesn't mean that everyone is cut out for all jobs: it means just the opposite. Trying to push everyone into the same mold is precisely why there are so many books on the market telling attorneys how to get out of practicing law. Yet leaving the field entirely isn't usually necessary. I want to show you how to STAY in your chosen field and choose—or create—a job that fits your skills and your life. One that fits your vision. Clarifying your vision, then taking the time to understand what a job entails and how it may align with your vision, skills and life, is one of the most important components of creating a successful and happy career journey.

I get it: practicing law requires continued devotion, education and work. But that doesn't mean you have to sacrifice the rest of your life! The idea is to live your full life, opening yourself up to experiences that present themselves to you—and then let those experiences help guide your career.

We all have those moments that trigger us to think about where we've been, where we are now, and where we're going in life. In the summer of 2017, I experienced one of these moments when I took my children on a tour of Vanderbilt University. The experience was lovely but pretty ordinary; yet as I flew back to Boise and started reflecting, I saw that this visit was pivotal. Looking at the world through my children's eyes prompted me to look back with utter clarity at my own experiences, education and life choices. I found myself asking: what could I have done differently? Where would I be if I had made choice *x* instead of choice *y?* I started thinking about where I started, where I've gone, where I am, and where I want to go next. And I realized it was time to begin exploring a new direction: my unhappiness at work had become significant enough that I knew it was time to leave.

Another pivotal experience revolved around the death of a close friend. She was a leader, a teacher, a person that made others happy and helped them find their own internal strength. She inspired anyone who was setting out to be a better person or take on new challenges. In remembering her and thinking of her legacy, I began to think of my own. I realized I want to be remembered as a person who used her strengths to help other people reach for and achieve their goals. I didn't think that would be how people remembered me if I died tomorrow—but that didn't mean I couldn't begin to change things in my life and try to make my vision a reality.

We all get caught up in making money and paying the bills. But at some point, you want to think of more than just the day-to-day grind. It's important that you *pause* a few times a year to look at your career and where you are going. Ask yourself: *What is my vision for my life? Am I being authentic? Am I still on the right path? Is my job a good fit for me?* Checking in with these questions will give you clarity, power and direction that will resonate throughout your necessary career choices. Remember, YOU are in charge of your life. You always have the option of making new decisions that lead you in new directions.

This book will help you develop concrete goals and a vision for your life that you can articulate to yourself and others. It will let you preview different career paths for attorneys, identifying aspects of each that can help you realize your vision or take you further away from it. On my website, www.lifestyleforlawyers.com, you'll find a workbook you can download with the questions we explore in this book, pulled together for your easy reference. My hope is you will use this resource to stay focused on what's important to you, even after you finish the book. Once you've connected to your internal vision and are familiar with the variety of career paths available today, then it's time to let your courage and confidence guide you to make the right choices throughout your life.

WHERE ARE YOU NOW ON YOUR LAWYER PATH?

Set aside some quiet time to reflect and write responses to the questions below.

Why did you go to law school? Be honest with yourself.

_____

_____

_____

_____

_____

What career steps or jobs have you taken since graduating from law school?

_____

_____

_____

_____

_____

Do you have a clear written vision for your life? _____

If you already have a vision, write it down here:

_____

_____

_____

_____

_____

What lifestyle benefits are important to you in your job?

_____

_____

_____

_____

_____

2

HOW CAN TECHNOLOGY HELP YOU TRANSFORM YOUR CAREER?

Each day, I read legal articles on the disruption of the legal industry, the challenges lawyers face because of changes in technology, and the potential impact of technology on the number of jobs available to attorneys. While many of the forecasts are grim, some are much more optimistic. In just the past year, I've started to see more predictions of an emergent legal industry that is collaborative, innovative and once again interested in problem solving. The changes in technology and the legal industry are creating new opportunities for lawyers. But it may not be a rosy picture for all attorneys: it will be those who embrace the changes who will succeed in the next decade.

As we all know, nothing is guaranteed or set in stone. Change can come—will come—and if you're not ready for it, you'll likely get left behind. Do you remember the first technology bubble and its explosion in the late 1990s? At the time, one company truly represented the 90s technology scene: AOL. In the mid-1990s, AOL was pretty much how all of us "dialed up" to the internet, and how most of us first started using email. The company seemed invincible, unstoppable. Yet just a few years later, it had lost most of its value. AOL's story shows how even technology leaders get left behind.

Steve Case was the CEO of AOL when the company was at the top of its game—and while it was in freefall. He went on to transform himself and his career. Today, Case is the CEO of Revolution, an investment firm in Washington, D.C., and the chairman of the Case Foundation, where he plays an integral part in Rise of the Rest, a nationwide effort to support entrepreneurs and startups around the nation.[2] In 2016 he wrote *The Third Wave*, which provides many insights regarding business disruption that apply perfectly to the legal industry.

"The Third Wave is an indispensable book for understanding the history of the Internet and preparing for what's next. Entrepreneurs looking to build truly transformational businesses should listen closely to Steve Case's insightful advice."

—Brian Chesky, cofounder and CEO, Airbnb

In his book, Case identifies the following conditions that set the stage for disruption in a given industry:

- Established businesses are being forced by financial challenges to do things differently.

- Technology has created the ability for companies and employees to work remotely and be connected globally; location is no longer paramount in business relationships.

- Venture funding companies are more interested in supporting startups.[3]

In my view, the legal industry meets all of Case's criteria for disruption:

- The U.S. legal industry has been doing things the same way for a long time. Yet law firms and legal departments have been under increasing financial pressure over the past fifteen years. Something will have to give: they can

11

no longer maintain the status quo and see the returns they want and need.

- Technology is changing—and will continue to change—the way attorneys live and work, with firms and individual attorneys becoming less tied to a physical location.

- Significant interest exists in funding entrepreneurs who want to disrupt the legal industry and make change happen.

The old-school legal industry is in existential jeopardy, or is set for a revolution, depending on how you look at things. But when I talk to attorneys at successful law firms, most fail to see how technology is truly disrupting their industry. They may realize they have fewer secretaries, or that they can now file cases electronically without going to the courthouse—but in their minds, the true disruption of the legal profession is not on the table. Honestly, many of them don't even seem to completely understand the threat. But almost all attorneys I talk to admit to feeling the financial pressures brought about by changes in the industry. They may even be trying to respond, yet most are only reacting, without a true understanding of what they're up against or where they're going.

This widespread lack of understanding of the new legal reality gives the advantage to lawyers who are willing to foresee changes and adapt. I see an increasing number of law firms and companies that thoroughly understand the threats and opportunities. They're changing—as fast as a stagnant industry will allow—to try and keep up.

The way we practice law is changing. You, too, can set yourself apart from the old guard by confronting the inevitable disruption, with all its possibilities and challenges. If you're a lawyer who understands technology, who likes change and innovation, this new legal market is rife with lifestyle benefits that suit your needs. It is also bringing new opportunities for flex careers.

LIFESTYLE TIP – *If you're interested in technology or flex careers and want more time for life outside of work, you might want to explore career paths in the alternative legal services industry. See Chapter 11.*

TECHNOLOGY CHALLENGES AND OPPORTUNITIES

Technology is revolutionizing the legal industry. The question is: will you get onboard and use it to revolutionize your career?

The industry has started to join forces with technology and business to create new legal solutions and delivery models. New ways of working remotely are surfacing within more traditional legal paths, and new legal careers and legal businesses are also emerging. Your job? Figuring out where you want to fit in this legal revolution. Ask yourself how you can use technology and the changing legal market to support your goals and lifestyle. For example: if you've always planned to have children and leave your career temporarily when the kids are young, consider whether a better course might be to stay in the legal market and work part-time remotely so you'll have more full-time opportunities when your kids are older. Is your major concern about the longevity of your career, and can you use technology or new legal businesses to distinguish yourself and become an expert in your field? What do you need to be a successful and happy lawyer?

One of the advantages technology brings to lawyers in the coming age of "new law"—at least for those who don't live in big cities and have no desire to move—is the ability to work remotely. In the past, if you wanted to make a name for yourself but lived outside of a major city, you were often forced to relocate, leaving friends and family to go where jobs were more readily available. Alternatively, you could choose to stay in your hometown near family and friends, but this often limited the type of legal career you could have and the income you could make. This is no longer the case.

With the evolution of technology, you no longer have to live in big cities to have a successful legal job. This fact has already had a significant impact on the life and legal career of many women I interviewed while writing this book—and me too—by allowing us to live and work outside of the main office, in the city we want to live in.

Before the internet, I would've never taken the job in India. Taking a break in my legal career would have been the end of it. But thanks to the internet (and other technological advancements), I was able to return to work while living overseas. When our family relocated back to the States in 2012, we moved to Boise, Idaho. Not because any particular company was there, but because that's where we wanted to live and raise a family. Boise fit our lifestyle choices. Another lifestyle benefit I cherish: being able to live where I want.

What lifestyle choices are most important to you right now? If you're having a child and need some time at home with your child, consider discussing with your boss whether they would let you work remotely after your maternity leave ends. Or maybe your spouse's job has relocated your family to another area of the country. In today's interconnected world, you may not have to leave your current job: before making a final decision, discuss the possibility of working remotely. Transportable jobs are more abundant than ever, and even more opportunities are on the horizon as business, technology and the law combine to create innovative new legal delivery solutions and careers.

LIFESTYLE TIP – *Many female lawyers are faced with the choice of staying in or leaving the practice of law when they have children. I was forced to make that decision. And in the years since, I've seen many women leave their careers behind when they have children. Unfortunately, I've also seen them desperately try to break back into the workforce when their children are grown, their marriages have ended in divorce or other financial reasons required their return. While it is always possible, it's not always easy to come back. I was fortunate to have taken only a short break from the practice of law. If circumstances permit, I would always recommend considering ways to stay in your chosen career when you have children—even if the work is part-time.*

Attorneys used to pick what type of law they wanted to practice, deciding whether they wanted to be a trial attorney, practice employment law, or perhaps work for a hospital. These days, that kind of choice may end up being a secondary decision for lawyers. The first and more important question may be: how is the security or longevity of my practice going to be affected by technology? At least, that *should* be your first question if you want to ensure your legal practice's success and growth over the next ten to twenty years.

Traditionally, lawyers were rewarded for the number of hours they billed. Today's lawyers, on the other hand, are increasingly rewarded for the ability to see how to do things differently. The business of law is opening up new workflows: lawyers are learning to produce more with less, and using artificial intelligence and automation of repetitive tasks to support their delivery of services and final products to clients.

Start thinking about how your current position might be challenged by the changes in technology, legal services, and delivery models that are coming onto the market. What can you do to keep up as the legal industry continues to evolve? What can you do to take advantage of changing industries and new opportunities to create your own legal path, so you can thrive and live the life you want? What past experience or skills do you bring to the table?

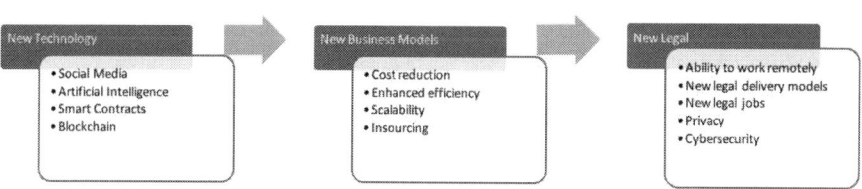

As you start thinking about what your path could look like, remember to think outside the box and look at your unique assets. My unique assets when I applied for my position with Cobra had nothing to do with my experience in eDiscovery, which was a big part of the job. In fact, at that time I didn't have any experience in large-scale eDiscovery. My assets in this case were my U.S. law license and my location: since I already lived in Chennai, the company didn't need to pay relocation costs or obtain a special work visa for my position.

What assets do you bring to the table that distinguish you from your peers? Don't overlook something that may set you apart, even if it is not a true legal qualification.

For example, if you live in an area known for leadership in a certain industry, such as healthcare, manufacturing, agricultural law, music or another specialty, don't overlook that as you plan your legal career. Even if that industry isn't your specialty now, you may find a place for yourself within it.

The new legal landscape will reward those with a variety of experiences. Even in failure. Perhaps you want to take a big step and start a new business within the new legal industry. Maybe you have an idea to build a legal-services delivery app—say, the Uber of the legal industry. But you worry: what if you give it a go and the idea flops? Even if it's a complete failure, as it very well might, you've still gained a valuable experience that can put you in the top minority of forward-thinking attorneys. You'll walk away with an expertise that few in your immediate community (or even larger community) can match.

> LIFESTYLE TIP – *If you're interested in technology, figure out how to work it into your legal career. Is there more training or certification that could help you? Take the time and, if necessary, money to explore how you can set yourself apart from your peers. You might be surprised to learn you have more knowledge and expertise than you thought. But don't forget: once you have that extra knowledge, you need to figure out how to let people know you've got it, and that you're ready to use it to help make their lives better. The last step can be particularly challenging for some women.*

Think about it: embracing such risks makes for a more compelling life story than if you stayed on as an associate at a 150-year-old firm you thought was secure and reliable, only to watch it file for bankruptcy. Think Dewey & LeBoeuf—an established law firm with more than a thousand lawyers worldwide that closed in 2012—or Howrey LLP, which had more than seven hundred attorneys across the globe and closed in 2011. I doubt that many of their associates anticipated that these long-standing law firms would ever close their doors, but they did. Today, holding tight to what feels certain and secure can carry its own risk.

TECHNOLOGY AND ETHICAL REQUIREMENTS

Changing technology brings with it more than just new opportunities. As the legal industry continues to evolve alongside changing technology, lawyers are being challenged with new ethical considerations. While you're focused on how to leverage and integrate technology to make your practice more efficient and value-driven, you also need to be sure you don't commit malpractice in the process.

Which brings me to ABA Model Rule 1.1. Attorneys have always needed to ask themselves whether they have adequate capabilities to represent a client. In addition to legal expertise, this now includes possessing the technical knowledge to represent a client. Pursuant to ABA Rule 1.1, Comment 8, in order for lawyers to "maintain their professional competence, they must 'keep abreast of changes in the law and its practice, including the *benefits and risks associated with the relevant technology*.'"[4] As of March 29, 2018, thirty-one states have adopted ABA Model Rule 1.1.[5]

Many authorities believe this duty will continue to shift as technology advances. In a recent article, Christian Mammen and Jason Lohr pointed out that "first, a lawyer should strike a balance between embracing beneficial new technologies and avoiding unnecessarily risky ones. There is ethical peril for both the first adopter and the Luddite."[6] As an attorney practicing law today, you should be able to recommend and use new technologies and advise clients when there are unnecessary risks involved in using new technologies.

There are plenty of instances of attorneys not being up-to-date on the latest technological advances—one such example is eDiscovery. Even if you don't consider yourself an eDiscovery attorney, you'll likely need to build some skills and knowledge in this area. Otherwise, you may find yourself in a position during discovery where you lack the technical background and competency to handle the process without bringing in an expert to assist you. Attorneys need to educate themselves on eDiscovery matters, and what federal and state judges expect in the courtroom. U.S. District Judge Xavier Rodriguez of the Western District of Texas told *Legaltech News,* in the fall of 2017, because they delegate eDiscovery matters to paralegals, vendors or associates, many attorneys feel "they need not be bothered with understanding the details."[7] Rodriguez noted that details overlooked by attorneys often include where and how much relevant data is stored, whether proportionality principles can be applied, and whether litigation holds have "been effectively put in place."[8]

The requirement of lawyers to be "competent" and "ethical" will continue to change. What about a lawyer's duty to supervise the work of non-lawyers? Mamman and Lohr suggest that there may arguably be an ethical duty for a lawyer to supervise a computer's work in the future.[9] Especially if that program is employing "Artificial Intelligence that is making decisions or performing work that is in the nature of delivering legal services—for example, preparing documents, making decisions about whether to produce certain documents, or the like."[10] And what about confidentiality arguments, when the computer-based program is provided by a third-party technology vendor on a single database? What if both the plaintiff and defendant are using the same technology provider?[11]

There are other Model Rules you should consider as well: ABA Model Rules 1.6 and 5.4. We know that Rule 1.6 (c) states that a lawyer shall make reasonable efforts to prevent the inadvertent or unauthorized disclosure of, or unauthorized access to, information relating to the representation of a client. Are you inadvertently putting your client's data at risk when you check emails at a restaurant—over a public Wi-Fi? What if you aren't adequately trained on the in-house eDiscovery software your firm uses to properly handle review and production? As our industry continues to evolve along with technology, attorneys will be challenged not only with staying abreast of the changing legal market, cybersecurity issues, eDiscovery, and the newest and greatest software changes—but also with how to stay in front of these changes and not commit malpractice.

Our changing economic world presents some extra challenges for the legal industry. ABA Model Rule 5.4 mandates that attorneys have professional independence, meaning that lawyers are prohibited from partnering with non-lawyers—and what once seemed clear-cut has become surprisingly murky. Some jurisdictions have issued rulings finding certain internet-based legal service providers in violation of this provision. So before you start a new business, implement a significant change in the way things are done in the industry, take a new job with a company instigating major change, or even send that tweet, do your research. You want to be sure you're in compliance with your ethical obligations.

Whether work is being done in your office, outside your office by an external vendor, or by a computer using artificial intelligence, as the lawyer handling the case you're the person supervising the work and the one who will represent to the judge the accuracy of the final product. To do this, you need to be sure you have a certain level of understanding of both the technology being used and the technology available. Take time to keep yourself and your career up-to-date on changes in technology: enroll in continuing legal education classes, online learning courses and webinars, and subscribe to news articles to stay informed on the latest developments. And when you learn about new developments in technology, always consider the possibilities and potential obstacles. Things to think about right now include the internet, cloud-based solutions, artificial intelligence, data protection, IoT and Wi-Fi. If you're unsure how to best protect your client's data or responsibly leverage new tools to win your case, consider outsourcing or hiring a well-qualified expert.

EXPLORE YOUR STRENGTHS AND ASSETS

It's time to start dreaming about how you want to be part of the legal revolution. You'll later use this exercise to begin building your vision in a way uniquely suited to your strengths and assets.

What are you good at that you enjoy? _____

_____

_____

What area of the country do you live in? How does your physical location affect your career as a lawyer? Are you willing or able to move?

_____

_____

_____

Is there a business or industry that is strong in your city? Healthcare? Automotive? Financial? Other?

_____

Do you have strong connections or experience in a special industry that you might use to distinguish yourself? _____

_____

_____

What are you interested in? This doesn't have to revolve around the law; this can also be a hobby or a group that you support.

_____

_____

_____

How do your contributions to, knowledge of, or involvement with the above interests and groups make you more interesting?

_____

_____

What part of your skills can be leveraged and how can you do this differently than others?

_____

_____

Technology - What do you like to do?	Computers Programming New technology development Social networking
What are you good at?	Writing Public speaking Managing others Persuasion
What are you interested in?	Running Church Yoga Community

3

HOW YOU CAN START TO SHAPE YOUR PATH

You probably consider yourself a diligent and successful person. You should, if you're reading this book: it's likely you've made it through law school, passed the bar, and held one or two jobs as an attorney. Not everyone can say that—you should be extremely proud of your accomplishments. But many of us who chose to go to law school and become lawyers are still unhappy. If this is where you find yourself, ask yourself why. Are you unhappy in your current position? Do you want to make more money? Do you crave more autonomy, more free time, more job security? Do you dream of working remotely or starting your own business? Do you feel like your job keeps you from being your authentic self? What's keeping you from finding happiness and success in precisely the ways you choose to define them?

You'll need to take some time determining what's holding you back and what lifestyle benefits you want; then you can set the ball in motion to achieve your goals. To find a legal practice that lets you have a life, and one that's financially rewarding. To have a job you're happy to wake up to every day.

Figuring all this out will take some work and imagination, but so will any career path today. Gone are the days when an attorney can sit back and be "fat and happy," content that their law practice will not change. Our parents may have worked the same job for their entire lives, but that time has come and gone. It's likely that during your career you'll have several different jobs; you may even decide to start your own business. A lawyer should look at a career path as just that: a path from one job to another, that over time builds a full and successful career. But keep in mind that this path may not be the straight climb up the corporate ladder you have envisioned. Sometimes the best, most fulfilling opportunity will present itself in an unexpected way—it may even seem like a step back in your career. When you figure out how to build on your life and career experiences, you can bring that accumulated knowledge along with you to deepen what you can offer to others.

I have found that as attorneys (and as people in general), we can often overthink. We can get so deep in the weeds of our case, project or life that it's hard to make the right choices. We can think ourselves into a corner, convincing ourselves of defeat before we even start. We may spend too much time meticulously perfecting every task—we want the "A," just like in school, thinking that the "A" will make everything else fall into place. Unfortunately (or perhaps fortunately), life is not exactly like law school.

Instead of overthinking, you want to step back and look at the bigger picture: from a career perspective, and also a personal one. Consider what type of career and life will make you happy. Not everyone is destined to be Johnnie Cochran—if you are and that's your goal, then make it happen. But it's crucial to reflect on your strengths and weaknesses in both your career and your personality, and align those with your career goals. You also want to consider the legal environment you're working in (or getting ready to enter) as you define goals and make career decisions. Think about how these factors can offer you momentum rather than resistance.

"You don't need to be a disciplined person to be successful. In fact, you can become successful with less discipline than you think, for one simple reason: success is about doing the right thing, not about doing everything right."

—Gary Keller and Jay Papasa [12]

Letting life pull you can be a powerful shift. The one time in my life where everything seemed to fall in place was when I lived in India: 2009–2011. During this period, life flowed and took me with it. It wasn't the period when I made the most money or earned the most accolades—but I let life take the lead and I followed. I felt at ease. I believed India was where I was meant to be at the time, and I was doing exactly what I was meant to be doing. I had the job I was meant to have, and I went to that job every day with the singular goal of doing that job well. I didn't dwell on the fact that I was no longer a partner in a law firm, or that I was working part-time making $35 per hour. I chose to enjoy where I was and what I was doing. I focused on what I was learning and where it could lead me.

Take a few minutes to think back about your life and where you've been. Try to remember a time when things just seemed to work: a time when you felt a sense of ease about your decisions, and the results were bountiful and good. It's exactly that type of contentment that leads one to an extraordinary career and life.

It's also important to realize that a big part of what ushers in this bliss, contentment—whatever you want to call it—is having the right mindset. Believing that things will work and focusing on the positives in your life will have a snowball effect. When you think back about a time in your life when things flowed with ease, I suspect that while you still had decisions to make, and you still had bad days, you brought the right attitude to the table. That attitude made all the difference.

After you've identified a past period of flow, consider how you might let life pull you in a similar way now. Think about how you can incorporate that natural momentum into your goals and career ambitions. For some of you, this may be a new process; it might take days or weeks to work through. If you already spend lots of time reflecting, this could take much less time.

IDENTIFY A TIME WHEN YOUR LIFE FLOWED

My life flowed when (capture details of this period of your life here):

_____

_____

_____

_____

_____

_____

_____

_____

_____

_____

_____

Take a few more minutes to reflect on how this period felt externally and internally, and how you interacted with others at the time. Many people have visual images that remind them of these special times. What you want to do is capture these feelings, images, sounds, smells—whatever you can visualize or imagine—and use them as tools to help shift your mind to the positive and optimistic outlook you had when you let life flow. Use them as shortcuts to get your head in the right space. They can get you out of the "bad head day," when you're being negative, judgmental or critical for no apparent reason. That is NOT where you want to be. That is NOT where good decisions will come from.

> LIFESTYLE TIP – *It's okay if you aren't 100% happy in your job. It isn't okay if you're unhappy and you're not exploring ways to improve your happiness factor. Even if you aren't ready to leave your current job, there are ways to improve your experience at work. Notice what happens when you spend just one day focusing on ways to make things better in your current situation.*

IDENTIFY WHAT IS IMPORTANT TO YOU

Now that you have identified a positive and optimistic feeling, let's set your goals for a bright, fulfilling career and life. This is a time when you can really look at what YOU want to be, a time to envision the best life that you can have. I want you to be completely SELFISH. What do you want your life to look like? What are the things that make you happy, that make you feel good? What would give you that same feeling of bliss that you captured in the first exercise of this chapter? What words help you describe this feeling of bliss? Love, power, community, spirituality, connection, control, family, money, or something else? Whatever it is, this is where you get to start writing down a list of what is most important to you. One rule: be honest. There is absolutely nothing wrong with saying that making money is important to you. There is also absolutely no reason to put down spirituality if that is not truly something that is important to you at this point in your life. In order to be happy and successful, you need to be honest with yourself; otherwise, you will still be in a pattern where you are doing something for someone else or based on what you think someone else wants. And we know that will not make anyone happy or successful. Also, it is important to look at your life as a whole in this exercise. Find the courage to look at yourself and what you want to be and let that be enough. Your personal life is important, so don't overlook the things that will make you happy and fulfilled in that area, too.

What is important to you?

1. _____

2. _____

3. _____

4. _____

5. _____

Next, I want you to take a more concrete look at what your life would look like if you made the things you most value a priority in your life. Imagine your life built around these words. Now think what your world might look like in the future if you let your life pull you toward these words. What would your life look like in a year, in three years, in five years, and in ten years. What is your life's plan?

One-year life vision

_____
_____
_____
_____
_____

Three-year life vision

_____
_____
_____
_____
_____

Five-year life vision

_____
_____
_____
_____
_____

Ten-year life vision

_____
_____
_____
_____
_____

Now that you have set some broad long-term goals, take a few moments and go back up to your one-year life vision. I'd like you to really dive into what your one-year vision would look like. Many people will start off by writing something like, "In one year I would like to have a job as . . ." or "In one year I would like to be living in . . ." or "In one year I want to start my own business . . ." This is a great place to start, but to really implement change and help you identify concrete steps to achieve your goals, we need to dig a little deeper. Take your one-year goals and identify what a typical day, week, and month would need to look like for you in relation to your goals. I like to do this by starting to think through what a typical day would look like for me and building from there.

Short-term goals:

Daily

- **Spirituality:** Meditate (5:00 to 5:30 a.m.)
- **Spirituality/Exercise:** Home yoga practice (5:30 to 6:30 a.m.) – 3 times per week
- **Family:** Get kids ready for school (6:30 to 7:30 a.m.)
- **Career:** Work (8:30 to 5:00 p.m.)
- **Family:** Dinner with family (6:00 to 7:00 p.m.)

Weekly

- **Career:** Take a one-hour webinar on topic of interest
- **Exercise:** Take a long run or hike
- **Family:** Do something special with my kids

Monthly

- **Family:** Have a special evening with my spouse/partner
- **Career:** Reflect on my career goals and path and reevaluate as needed
- **Financial:** Evaluate finances
- **Self-Care/Exercise:** Get a massage

This is the way I approach my reflection, but you can do it any way that works for you. You may find it more logical to list the category and then make weekly, monthly, and yearly goals under each category that is important to you. The important component of this exercise is to get as detailed as possible, in writing. This will be a place you will want to come back to regularly for inspiration and to monitor your progress. It is equally important that you view these goals and visions as a living plan. These visions for your future are likely going to change as you start working toward your plan. This is to be expected. Don't overlook a great opportunity just because you didn't plan on it. I have provided two sets of pages that you can use for your notes.

Daily

_____
_____
_____
_____
_____
_____
_____

Weekly

_____
_____
_____
_____
_____
_____

Monthly

_____
_____
_____
_____
_____
_____

Yearly

_____
_____
_____
_____
_____
_____

OR

Category (_____)

_____
_____
_____
_____
_____
_____

Category (_____)

_____
_____
_____
_____
_____
_____

Category (_____)

_____
_____
_____
_____
_____
_____

Category (_____)

_____
_____
_____
_____
_____
_____

Now that you have identified what is important to you and what that might look like in your day-to-day world, we can start the real work on setting goals and putting together a plan for how to achieve these goals.

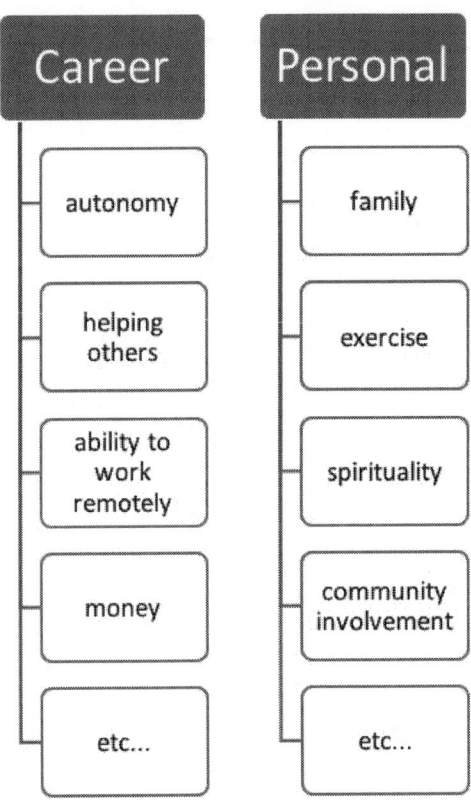

4

IDENTIFY YOUR CAREER GOALS, YOUR VISION, AND YOUR PATH

In Jason Isbell's song, "If We Were Vampires," he sings about our limited time here on earth and how this changes his perception of what is important. What a great way to look at life! To each of us what is important will likely be different and that is okay and entirely the point.

Our time here matters and we can make the most of it when we live from our core with intention. Before you can be successful, at peace, happy, and inspiring in your life and career you need to know who you are and who you are in your legal profession. To do this, the first step is to take responsibility for your own success and start creating the life that you want.

> "We broadcast what we are, and others pick it up. When Gandhi said 'My life is my message,' he was speaking for us all."
>
> —Eknath Easwaran

I have always found that my life goes much better when I rely on the "je ne sais quoi," a somewhat indescribable sense of inner direction. For some, this indescribable something may come in the form of a conversation with God; for others, a little inner voice or a sign. The exact identification of where the instruction or feeling is coming from is not what matters. What matters is that you are listening and following that instinct. That you are conversant with your inner voice and taking a good look at what it might be saying to you. If you do, you can use that "voice," "gut feeling," "direction" or "guidance" to inspire you and help build your life! Let it help you come up with your own vision, remembering that no one else has the same vision that you have. Focus on

"Your vision of where or who you want to be is the greatest asset you have. Without having a goal it's difficult to score."

—Paul Arden[13]

what moves and inspires you, even if it means going against the grain.

CREATE YOUR VISION AND YOUR STORY

When I first got started in the legal world, I had no idea that I would one day be living in India and working in eDiscovery for a start-up company in a start-up industry. Yet in 2010, I was interviewing at an International Legal Process Outsourcing company in their Chennai offices. At this time, eDiscovery and LPOs were the new buzzwords in the legal publications, and if you were practicing law at this time you probably received one or two emails from people in India asking if they could help you do legal work (emails which you quickly deleted). Nor did I ever think I would one day be writing a book. But as I have moved through my professional career and applied the principles I've outlined in this book, I have been able to make the necessary adjustments and choices to adapt to changes in my career and circumstances. I'm always ready to accept new opportunities, even ones I haven't anticipated. With each career, I've created a successful stepping stone to the next leg of my career. Yes, change can be scary, really scary! Change can also be fantastic and freeing and just what you need to get to the next better phase of your life and career. But never forget to take your past experience with you and build on those experiences.

If you are not happy in your current position or career,

something as simple (and as difficult) as change may be just the thing that you need to grow. Now is your time to reflect and decide whether the needed change is a physical change in your job, a mental change in your attitude, or both.

You always have a choice.

LIFESTYLE TIP – *Yoga, breathing techniques, and meditation can help eliminate negative brain chatter, open the mind to new ways of thinking, ease anxiety and increase focus and concentration. Check out www.lawyersandyoga.com for an introduction to different types of yoga and meditation to help lawyers cope with stress at work. You may find you don't need to change jobs, you just need to change your mindset. Learn how you can use traditional yoga techniques in your daily legal practice and become more effective, efficient and happy.*

You don't have to stay in a job that you hate. You don't have to drive a fancy car. In fact, you don't have to do most things!

If you've always wanted to make a certain salary . . . if you've always wanted to live in a certain house . . . if you've always wanted to work in a certain industry . . . if you've always wanted to work for a law firm . . . if you've always wanted to work for a judge . . . if you've always wanted to work for a nonprofit . . . then make it happen! Incorporate it into your vision for your life and own that goal.

In order to be in control of your life, you have to make a conscious effort to select a path that matters to you. It is very unlikely that you will be happy if you are not on the right path. Once you've made a conscious choice of which path you want to be on, you will have the sense of ownership and power that you'll need to make the right choices. If you are making choices that are taking you down a path you have thoughtfully chosen for the right reasons, it'll generally be a positive and powerful experience.

This is the time to start making the changes you need to be happy. This is the time to stop playing the unhappy victim who is in a dead-end job, who has the horrible boss, who doesn't make enough money. This is the time where you get to own your power, make your own choices, set some boundaries, and start enjoying your life.

I recently participated in an ACEDS webinar entitled "Burning Career Questions," which was hosted by Jared Coseglia, Founder & CEO of TRU Staffing Partners. Jared finished up the webinar by asking the audience how they prepared for an interview, and, of course, most people came back with the traditional response of "I research the company." I think most of us have been trained or told that this is the correct response (whether we take the time to research the company or not). But Jared offered a different take. For him, as someone with a theater background and as the CEO of a staffing company, it is the applicant's "story" that distinguishes them from the crowd of other people being interviewed. "Interviewing is good storytelling!" he said.

This really hit me as being a valid point. Telling the story of yourself, how you've gotten to where you are in your life and career, and where you want to go are what will really distinguish you, whether you are in an interview or just trying to establish yourself as a new associate at a law firm. What Jared was recommending was more than just telling what you did at your job; good storytelling requires more thought and insight than that. It requires vision and something personal about yourself, something that people (at least some people) might be able to identify with and remember. Be inspiring!

Consider Jared's advice to learn your own story and learn how to tell it. You've already taken the time to examine what you want from life and a career. (I suspect few people have taken this time, so therefore you will have already set yourself apart.) Now reflect deeply on what you have done, how you have done it well, and how you could make it better in the future. You might even realize something new about yourself. Maybe the reason you didn't make partner is because it wasn't a good fit for you. And maybe the partners realized that, but you hadn't yet taken the time to look critically at yourself, your skills, your life interests, and goals. So, you couldn't see it. Or maybe you still believe that being a partner at a law firm would be a good fit, but with some reflection you can recalibrate and improve on your story and your skills to make that happen. Life has a way of sending us signals to help us grow and improve ourselves; we just have to be willing to listen to these signals and take the needed steps to change.

Isn't understanding the story of someone and their strengths what most employers, companies, and law firms want? When I was a senior supervisor at an international company with more than 170 employees, I know that is what I wanted to see! I was initially attracted to hire the person that could explain to me why they were interviewing for the position, why they thought they would be a good fit for the position, and what excited them about the position. They could answer with clarity, "Who are you?" and "Who are you at this point in your career in this legal market, and who do you want to be?"

It is important to provide experience that supports your story and put it within a context the company will care about. How have your prior work and life experiences put you in a position that will enable you to make the company stronger, more productive, and better positioned in the marketplace? In other words, relay the story of your professional career and articulate how your experiences would provide a valuable resource for the company.

Consider your story up to this point and now think where you want it to go. What is your vision for the future? Do you feel you have the freedom to move or do you feel stuck in a position without choices? If you feel you are stuck without options, don't immediately make a new choice. This is the time to reflect and realize there are infinite possibilities and steps to lead you toward a goal. What you need to do is figure out a whole set of steps that will lead you on your path, the path that fits. Use the exercises you completed in the last chapter and look at where you have been and want to go. Begin to explore a vision that reflects and broadcasts your authentic self, a vision you want to embody on a daily basis in your career and your personal life.

CREATIVE QUESTIONS TO EXPLORE YOUR VISION

Some people find this process difficult. I know that it was sometimes hard for me to really articulate what it was that I wanted and build a vision. One exercise that you may find helpful to get at the core of what you want is to ask questions to help define your goals. There is something powerful about a good question. It can be the tool you use to initiate conversations with strangers, put others at ease, and explore your inner world. And asking the right question at the right time can be life changing.

Lawyers are trained to ask questions and listen attentively to the response. We do it daily in our job, whether in a meeting with a potential new client, deposition, voir dire, cross examination—the list goes on. There is a distinct and valuable skill to these types of questions we ask in our daily work, but the questions we will explore here are different. We will still be focused on asking the right questions and listening actively to the answers, but these questions will be more strategic in nature. And, in most instances, you will be asking the questions of yourself—not someone else.

The purpose of these questions is to help you look at your life as a whole: where you've been, where you're going, how you can get to where you want to go, and ultimately how you would like others and yourself to view your life and your career. For most people these questions will require that you weigh long-term goals with the potential risks and costs (whether measured in time, money, or something else).

First, think back to some goals you've already set for yourself in your one-, three-, five-, and ten-year visions. For each one, ask yourself the following questions:

- Does this course of action advance my interests?

- Do I have a calling, or a bigger purpose, aligned with this goal?

- Does it feel right—is it important to my core values?

- Do I have the passion and perseverance to not only start down this path, but to finish it?

- What will I define as being "successful" on this journey?

- Do I have access to the tools to make this goal happen? (Be realistic here.)

- Have I considered the costs, benefits, and risks?

- Are there alternative ways to achieve the same goal?

- How will this affect my friends and family?

- How will this affect my legacy and how others perceive me as a person?

Now step back, take off your conservative lawyer hat, and ask these same questions from a different vantage point. Imagine that you have already created your new widely successful business (or landed the job at the big law firm or are working from home with your kids in the next room). Imagine what a day in this life might be like. Let yourself daydream for a few minutes and try to appeal to your imagination, greatness, and sense of destiny! Set your sights as high as you can go or would like to go.

Ask yourself:

- What am I doing?

- What does my new company or new position look like?

- How does it feel to be in my new position?

- What am I known for?

- What am I most proud of?

Then dream further:

- What would it be like to run a $50-million company?

- What would it be like to speak to a crowd of ten thousand people?

Use these questions to craft your own vision and story and make it original. Force your brain to think of things differently—think of your job, your goals, your aspirations, and yourself differently! Would any of these goals or dreams change if you knew that failure was not a possibility?[14]

Now answer the following questions.

What was my first job out of law school?

_____

_____

_____

What other jobs have I held since law school?

_____

_____

_____

What is an instrumental project that I participated in (or created)?

_____

_____

_____

Why was that project important or meaningful to me?

_____

_____

_____

Where do I see myself going with my career? (This is a condensed version of the question from the last chapter where I asked you to look at your whole life vision; here we are focused on just your career.)

_____

_____

_____

What is the best way to get there?

_____

_____

_____

Where do I want to be in my career in one year?

_____

_____

_____

Where do I want to be in my career in three years?

_____

_____

_____

What are my realistic short-term goals? (One-month, three-month, and six-month goals)

_____

_____

_____

Looking back at my career one day, what would I like to see?

_____

_____

_____

As you're starting to get some goals down on paper, it is important to remember this is a long-term commitment and process. To succeed you'll need to have daily focus on your goals and what you can control. You'll also need to keep three important things in mind: 1) you need to bring the right attitude every day, 2) you cannot control everything, and 3) never forget to be prepared.

Your attitude is the foundation of everything, and as you think about your goals and your path, it's important to maintain a positive mindset about work in general. You hear so many people complain about going to work or having to go to work, yet I would say we should embrace the opportunity to be able to work. Be thankful every day that you have a job to go to and that you *can* work. You won't be able to find a job that makes you happy until you first adopt this mindset. From here, you can then move forward to create your vision of a happy work life.

A positive attitude will also help you accept that you can't control everything that happens around you—no one can—and move on to make the best of the reality you're working with. How can you shift your mindset to your advantage?

> LIFESTYLE TIP – *I really meant what I said about yoga and meditation being a great tool to get your life on the right course, help you create a positive mindset, and learn how to visualize what your life can look like. If you think that getting up and going to work tomorrow is going to be hard, it probably will be hard. If you think, "I am really learning a lot preparing for this trial, what a great experience this is, I am so lucky to have this opportunity," the experience of getting up and going to work tomorrow is going to feel much different. It's important to learn how to have positive brain chatter. Again, try integrating yoga and meditation into your daily life. Either through an online service or with a local yoga or meditation studio. You may also want to take a look at The Grit Project,[15] a program supported by the ABA to help women to develop a growth mindset.*

That's where being prepared comes in handy. You don't want to miss that unexpected opportunity, because you aren't ready to go when it presents. So get that extra accreditation, attend that conference to make new contacts and build your résumé, or join that board.

About two or three times a year, I would like you to sit down and spend some solid time thinking about where you are in your life, where you are in your career, and how it all comes together. Ask, how is the legal market changing? What new companies have come into the legal industry? Why have these new legal companies entered the market? Is there another type of legal service provider or solution that would be helpful to my clients? What are my goals in my personal life? Have my personal goals changed? How could my personal goals be changed to make my life more fulfilling, easier, or better? As you can see, this process is not just about your personal life or your work life; they are both essential and interconnected parts.

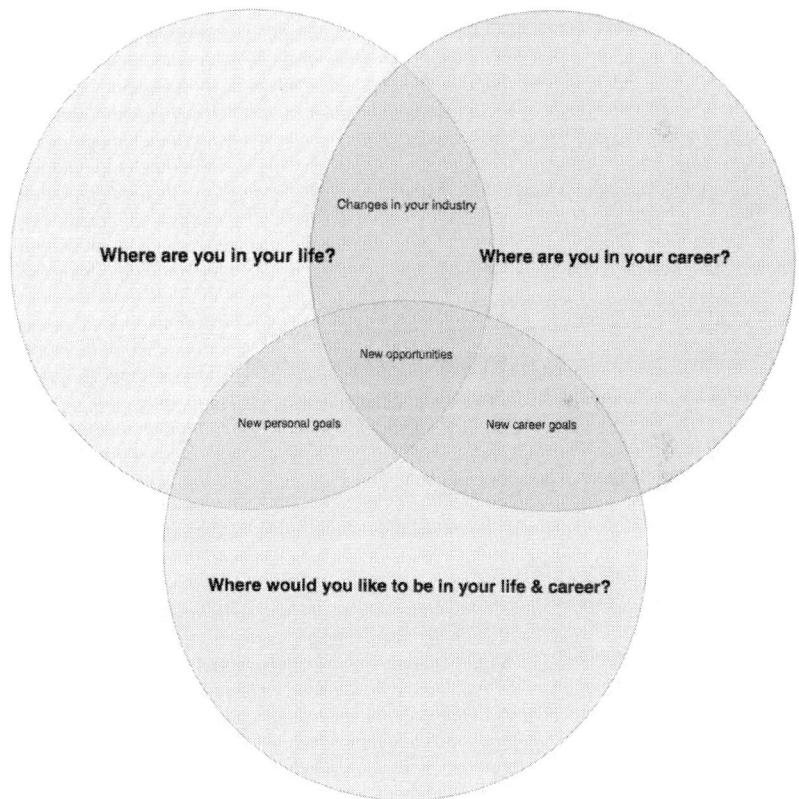

SET YOUR VISION FOR YOUR LEGAL CAREER PATH

Think through the following:

1. Look at your interests and skills and consider how these can be used to bring value to your legal career.

2. Reflect. Take time to reflect before taking action. What does your inner voice say? What does the legal market-place look like today? What are the career options in front of you? Are there other alternative career options that you have not considered yet?

3. Consider bringing other people into the picture to help you clarify your goals. Depending on where you are in your career, this could be a parent, friend, spouse, men-tor, career counselor, or trusted colleague.

4. Focus on finding out what type of career will work best with your personality. This is where you identify what lifestyle benefits are important to you. Are you com-fortable working a "9-to-5" job in an office with little flexibility or would you be willing to take less money to work from home or for a more flexible company?

5. Focus on the questions that the legal industry is asking. Read articles from other attorneys online, see what CLE subjects are being offered and try to start spotting new legal trends or hot topics.

6. What are the changes that you see coming in the legal industry?

7. Is there one part of the legal industry you believe is best suited for you? (We'll explore this question more in sec-tion 2.) Which of the following paths are you currently most drawn to?

   a. Working for a corporation
   b. Working at a traditional law firm
   c. Working in a new legal job

8. What would your fallback plan look like?

Now get some thoughts down on paper.

What do you want your focus to be as an attorney?

_____

_____

Are you currently in your desired position as an attorney or do you need to make a move to a different job?

_____

_____

What are the challenges that you are facing in your current position? Why are you happy or not happy there?

_____

_____

What experiences do you have that you can bring to the table to distinguish yourself in your current job or use to help you get a new job?

_____

_____

_____

Are there other career paths that you have not considered before? Think big here. Get out of your comfort zone.

_____

_____

What skills do you have that might set you apart from other lawyers?

_____

_____

Thinking ahead, what career step will be useful to take you to a larger career goal down the road?

_____

_____

Take out your résumé and reflect on your accomplishments to date. What have you excelled at? What have you enjoyed doing most?

_____

_____

Once you've answered this question, take out and update your résumé to add any recent accomplishments. If you don't have any to add, consider setting a short-term goal like writing an article or joining a new legal committee so you do have something new to include. Start making this a regular habit, even if you are not looking for a job.

Does your résumé highlight your education and work history in a way that tells a compelling story of where you have been and where you are going?

_____

_____

If it needs work and you hate writing résumés (like me) or lack confidence in the result, consider hiring an expert to help. In my experience, having a professionally reviewed and written résumé can be empowering. It gives you that extra comfort that your résumé is ready to go—now you can focus on landing the job instead of wasting brain power on a résumé.

What real world experiences do you bring to the table that can translate to your career and career goals? Focus on positive stories where you succeeded in solving a problem.

_____

_____

What organizations are of particular interest to you that might help you become more engaged in the legal market you want to establish yourself in?

Women's organizations _____

Technology organizations _____

State bar groups _____

Defense attorney groups _____

Corporate counsel groups _____

Cybersecurity organizations _____

eDiscovery organizations _____

Others _____

_____

_____

Don't forget to spend some real time on this chapter. Thinking these questions through is important and will give you the power to tell your authentic story, the story that you're really passionate about, the story that inspires you and others. When you've nailed it, you'll know it and so will others. And remember, you don't have to do this alone. Work with whomever you need to set your vision and career path into play. When you're ready, take a stab at pulling it all together and putting your vision for your career and life into a succinct statement. What does success mean to you?

MY VISION

_____

_____

_____

_____

5

DEFINE WHAT YOU DO BEST IN YOUR LIFE AND WORK

Now that you have a vision for your life and your career, it is important to begin taking steps to move toward it. Wherever you are in your career, if you're using the skills and talents that come easiest to you, it's likely you're doing your job well and that you're a happy, pleasant person to be around. Moreover, I would say you're being an excellent attorney. And by excellent, I don't mean the best litigator in your city. I define excellence as the best attorney for you, your family and your client. Be authentic. Be focused on how to make your job fit into your life, needs, and strengths rather than shaping yourself to fit the job. If you can do that, you'll be a much better attorney than you could ever be while trying to be something you're not.

It's important to know both your limitations and your best qualities. From that realistic awareness, though, it's essential to focus on the BEST qualities and use those to build your career. Because why would you want to focus on your limitations? Focus instead on what comes naturally to you, developing those strengths further and building your career from that place of strength. I promise if you do that you'll have more clients, more success for your clients, more happiness, more enjoyment, and ultimately more money than if you focus on limitations or try to build a career from an inauthentic place. Find the sweet spot in your life. Things will start to flow.

So how do you do this? You can try to decipher that sweet spot by looking at your current job and how you're performing, and then evaluate what job or skills look like the best fit for your personality and natural talents.

HOW TO DETERMINE WHAT YOU DO BEST

Out of all of the female attorneys that I have worked with and interviewed over my career, the happiest and most successful are the ones who have learned how to incorporate their personal interests and skills into their career.

Let's start with what first comes to mind. What have you always been really good at? Writing, public speaking, networking, yoga, building things? Write down the top five things that you do really well.

THINGS I DO WELL

1. _____

2. _____

3. _____

4. _____

5. _____

Now let's explore and try to name the things that you may not immediately realize you do well. In order to figure this out, I want you to take some time and think through what other skills you may have that you haven't yet considered. You may also want to ask your family or friends what they see as your strengths or talents. You might be surprised by their answers. And you might be surprised to find out that all or most of the people you speak with perceive you as having a certain strength or skill that you hadn't realized you possessed. List these additional items below.

ADDITIONAL THINGS THAT I AM GOOD AT

1. _____

2. _____

3. _____

4. _____

5. _____

If you really want to dig deep you can take a personality or aptitude test, such as the Caliper Profile, Myers-Briggs, or Gallup StrengthsFinder. These tests may help you feel more confident about your skills and/or may help you find out that you have overlooked an area where you are in fact particularly strong.

USE YOUR STRENGTHS IN YOUR JOB

Now that you've identified what you're good at, you'll need to find ways to apply these strengths and interests in your current job. If your strength is writing and you've not been writing anything but form pleadings since you started practicing law, consider writing articles for publication in a journal. If your strength is public speaking and you've yet to see the inside of a courtroom or participate in a trial, volunteer to speak at a CLE or upcoming conference in your industry. If you're a yoga teacher, consider teaching a yoga class. If you're not currently working or if your current job does not allow you to utilize your strengths, look for volunteer opportunities that do: become a member of a board, take a pottery class, volunteer with a local group, teach a Sunday school class or be a volunteer at a local school. Using your natural strengths in your daily activities will empower you, give you confidence, and make you happier. You may even find that others notice this and that new doors and opportunities start opening.

KNOW WHAT YOU NEED

What are the best parts of your current job? It may be that you get to work from home full-time, or that you only have to be in the office four days a week. Maybe quality of life and extra vacation are more important to you than a big home and big paycheck. Maybe you love your job because you get to work for a non-profit organization in an industry that is important to you. To find the right job fit, it is essential to know what you want from a job. It's equally important to understand the needs of your employer. That will help get you started out on the right foot.

For many of my friends and colleagues, flexibility in work schedule and location is their biggest concern. If having such flexibility is really important to you, then you need to know that up front, and be honest with yourself and your current or prospective employer.

Many employers are increasingly seeing flexible schedules and working remotely as extremely reasonable requests. My children have grown up with two parents that have worked from home the entire time they have been old enough to notice. It's completely normal for them, and will be normal for increasing numbers of kids. This type of flexibility is growing in the legal field, and the ability to work outside of normal 9-to-5 in-office work hours will likely be an attractive component of the job for many female attorneys.

Increased flexibility isn't the only change coming, of course. With advancements in technology we're entering a new business and legal age where some of the more repetitive and boring aspects of the job from days past will be increasingly taken over by technology. This shift will allow for forward-thinking law firms and companies to enable and reward more creativity and professional development from the lawyers who can fully understand and utilize the technology impacting the legal profession.

If you're the type of person who wants to innovate—creating a new way of working or a new delivery system, or whatever that would look like for you—a position with a forward-thinking law firm or legal department that offers the freedom to experiment will be a necessity for your growth within your position and your career.

Increasing flexibility and automation are bringing new opportunities for you to have a job you truly love that provides what you need and fits into your life. Add to this the fact that there are more legal jobs available today focused around industries and ideas that inspire the imagination, offering a creative atmosphere with the potential to bring out the best in lawyers. Flexibility and room for creativity will become more and more attractive to prospective employees, and employers who don't already embrace these things will need to make some changes in order to continue bringing in the best of the best. This means that the number of forward-thinking firms and companies for you to consider will grow.

Finding the right fit will likely take additional time. But finding that right fit with a firm or company that appreciates and understands your mindset will reward you throughout your career—and reward the company as a whole. So make sure that your current job or a potential job aligns with your vision! Determine what must-haves you need for a job to fit within your life and vision, and always go back to them. These are important! Don't apply for a job or remain in a job that doesn't meet these criteria. Don't automatically take the highest-paying job, if the rest of the job doesn't meet your expectations and fit with your vision and must-haves.

Now it is time to set your eye on the prize and put your essential lifestyle benefits down on paper. Sit with all that you've reflected on up to this point. You may want to consider things like income, benefits, and flexible hours. Or you may be more focused on what type of industry you are working in, the type of people that you are working for, autonomy, the option to work remotely, attend industry conferences, growth/learning opportunities, along with the ability to write and publish articles.

Identify the components of your current or future job that you consider essential lifestyle benefits:

1. _____

2. _____

3. _____

4. _____

5. _____

HOW TO SET YOUR GOALS TO LAND THE RIGHT JOB

You've identified where you're at in your career, you've set a vision for yourself, identified your strengths, and identified what components of a job are most important to you. It is now time to set a plan and start taking steps to realize your goals. I like to think of a big-picture goal first and then set the smaller near-term goals that will help lead me to my ultimate destination. So, for example, if your goal is to start your own consulting practice, your plan on paper might look something like this:

Big-Picture Goal: Start a consulting business in one year
Smaller Near-Term Goals:

1. Put together a business plan

2. Build a website

3. Start writing and submitting articles for publication in the top journals

4. Attend a conference on the specific area of law I will be targeting for consulting work

5. Set three speaking engagements at local and high-profile conferences

6. Keep going . . .

You can start listing these below or you might want to get a separate goal journal to continually add to and rework!

Big-picture goal: _____
Smaller near-term goals:

    1. _____

    2. _____

    3. _____

    4. _____

    5. _____

    6. _____

Big-picture goal: _____
Smaller near-term goals:

    1. _____

    2. _____

    3. _____

    4. _____

    5. _____

    6. _____

Big-picture goal: _____
Smaller near-term goals:

1. _____

2. _____

3. _____

4. _____

5. _____

6. _____

Once you have a nice long list of near-term goals, go back over them and think about what you're most excited about and what absolutely needs to be done. Then divide your goals into two lists: goals that excite you and goals that must be done (and most likely completed in a particular order). There will always be some goals that aren't as exciting as the rest. But I've found in my own life and through working with others that once we dive in and start working toward these goals, we frequently discover we don't mind the work involved as much as we thought we would and that we feel more pleasure and accomplishment when the goal is achieved.

Now, prioritize your goals so they are manageable. What do you believe will really work? And which goals are most accessible to you right now? Which ones are still manageable but might be harder to reach? As you prioritize, I recommend that you rotate between the goals that excite you and the goals that just need to be completed.

After you achieve a goal, mark it off of the list and then reevaluate what's left. Don't just assume that the next listed goal is what you should tackle next. You may be able to do this in many instances, but depending on how long it took you to meet your first goal and whether other circumstances have changed, you may need to add, remove, or adjust certain goals, and prioritize what's left.

As you work toward these goals, remember it is completely fair to ask for and utilize help in this process. This is not law school. If you have access to an assistant or need to hire someone to help you, then put those people in place to help make your goals a reality. If you're going to present at a big speaking engagement and you're nervous or unsure about the presentation, consider hiring a speaking coach to give you some tips, help you prepare your speech, and rehearse before the big event. If you don't have the skills or time to build that website, hire a website developer to do it for you. It'll be money well spent.

Goals that excite me!   Goals that need to be done!

1. _____   _____

2. _____   _____

3. _____   _____

LIFESTYLE TIP – *Many successful people get considerable help along the way. If something is really important to you and your career, but you're feeling uncertain or might perform better with a little extra help, there is absolutely nothing wrong with getting some help from a professional. Hire an editor, or even another attorney, to read that brief before you submit it to the court. Get a speaking coach to help you with your closing argument or help you dial in your client pitch. People do this every day; no one can do everything perfectly. Know what you do well, and what could use a little extra polishing. It'll be well worth the money and you'll likely save time and decrease some of your stress in the process.*

WAYS TO IMPROVE

As you dedicate yourself to reaching your goals, don't forget to keep improving other areas of your life, too. Earlier I said you should focus on what you are good at. And you should! But I would recommend that you also take advantage of whatever opportunities present themselves, such as those your employer may offer to increase your knowledge base through new challenges at work, certification training or continuing legal education. Additionally, you should continue spending time in personal reflection and do any necessary work adjusting your own perception of yourself, if needed. Back to how important it is to have a positive growth mindset: Eliminate the negative talk!

I think most of us have a distorted perception of ourselves and our abilities in at least one area. For me, I had a deep-rooted belief that I was not a good speaker or writer. But then I started reading what others wrote and listening to how others spoke more closely and I started questioning that belief about myself. Once I stepped back and figured out why I thought that way, I was able to change that negative perception of myself. I learned that I simply don't like to speak on things I'm not passionate about. Like many of you, I was first introduced to public speaking in law school, where I was repeatedly asked to speak on subjects I didn't truly understand or feel strongly about. For three years I was constantly being placed in the position of speaking on subjects that left me uninspired, confused and nervous. Not the best place to start. After law school, though, I was able to start speaking on subjects that I connected with and understood deeply. I remember the first case that I presented in court. I had worked on that case for over a year. I knew it, understood the people, and cared about the outcome. And wow, what a difference that made in my ability to speak publicly and with passion.

My point? Don't let your own perception stop you from doing something without first making sure it's valid. And even if you do determine a personal limitation you associate with yourself is valid, don't turn down a project just because you think it might be a little difficult. Take projects that require you to stretch beyond your current capabilities and work at them. When you do this, one of two things will likely happen: You might do a great job, leading to greater respect from your peers and, more importantly, growth in your own skills, self-respect and self-esteem. Or, you might not have the best experience. But in the process, you'll learn a great deal and be better equipped to handle the next demanding project.

Always consider what expertise you can develop to bring to your job or your law firm to provide an innovative solution to a common process. Is there some new technology your firm could use in court? Is there a new legal app on the market you could introduce to the office? Research these new solutions and consider pitching them to your supervisor, the managing partner, or the general counsel. You'll expand your knowledge, build your reputation, and create new opportunities.

Finally, explore how you relate to others and what brings a positive response in your interactions in and outside work. Note what image or energy you're sending to the outside world and then ask yourself if this is what you want to radiate. If not, recalibrate and do your best to relate to others in a more intentional way. Shifting this energy will improve yourself, your life, and the lives of those around you.

6

DISTINGUISH YOURSELF IN YOUR JOB AND YOUR LIFE

We are all unique and we all have something that we can offer to life and to each other. Figuring out how to uncover that unique part of yourself and how best to develop that uniqueness in your everyday life is vital to living a happy and full life.

By now, you should be ready to make some changes in your life. The change may be just one thing, like learning to believe that you are unique or valuable. The most important thing that you can do at this point is to stay committed to yourself, your plan, and your vision. Be SELFISHLY MINDFUL and AUTHENTIC every day. If you can do just this one thing, it'll be a life-changing accomplishment for yourself and everyone you encounter.

> *As human beings, our job in life is to help people realize how rare and valuable each one of us really is, that each of us has something that no one else has— or ever will have—something inside that is unique to all time. It's our job to encourage each other to discover that uniqueness and to provide ways of developing its expression.*
>
> *—Mr. Rogers[16]*

THOUGHTFUL PREPARATION

When I interview female attorneys about their careers, I always ask them about the most stressful part of their job. Not surprisingly, almost all of them indicate that they started to have difficulties with the high-pressure demands of their careers and the law firm culture, especially when they started having kids. With or without kids, these pressures can be draining; working as a female attorney, especially in certain environments, often brings with it a fair amount of stress. Sometimes that stress might be enough to warrant making a change in your career and sometimes it might be something you want to work through as best as you can. Even if you do change positions, the chances are you will still find yourself overwhelmed at times. Being mindful of what you are doing each day and about your goals and vision can go a long way in helping to quiet some of this stress.

How do I remain mindful? For me, it works well to start out the day with a short meditation session. Meditating between five to fifteen minutes is usually enough to calm my mind and bring the right perception to the table. And by perception, I don't mean just my own; I mean the perception of others as well. If you do something from a calm, relaxed, and controlled state of mind, your actions will be perceived by others as strong and powerful. If you're exhausted or frazzled, then you're in a weak and vulnerable space and your actions will be perceived by others as weak.

At other times, my go-to mind-reset activity is yoga, running or biking. But these are not the only options. Do what works for you. The most important aspect will be to engage in regular activities that help you come away with a positive mindset.

Ask yourself, how are my actions going to be received and what are my true end goals? Taking a few moments to remind yourself of your goals and the process needed to get there will help you focus your actions (and inactions) in the most effective, efficient manner. To stay connected to your goals, you may find it helpful to write out your thoughts after you pray, meditate, or reflect. Some people will find comfort in a mantra that they go back to throughout the day or when they are stressed. It's up to you to develop a system that works for you. But it's imperative that you have a consistent plan in place to keep focused on your goals in order to achieve them. Something to get you through the hard times.

Throughout your day, take the time to think before you respond. So often people are in a hurry to do as much as they can in the shortest time possible, and this seems particularly true for attorneys: The more I can get churned out the quicker the better. I can get home earlier, I can get more billable hours, I can get in a round of golf before I go home, the list continues. But remember, part of being happy is figuring out what your sweet spot is, what keeps you going and gets you excited. If you can let life pull you in this direction, you'll no longer need to always churn out the most work possible, but can focus on responding to others in a thoughtful and compassionate manner. If you're tapped into this authentic level of commitment and communication, most people will respond in kind and remember you and want to work with you. This will likely have a snowball effect where you'll be engaged with people that are sending you the work you like to do and you're doing a better job at this work.

To recap: Set your mind for the day and work within your sweet spot. Be mindful of your interactions with others, communicating in a thoughtful and respectful manner and also always keeping your end goals in sight. Oh, and pick your battles! I first learned this lesson in Parenting 101, but I've only recently learned to apply this to my career. Once I added this step into my thought process, certain decisions became much easier. For example, if you serve on a board, you might ask, why am I on this board? If the board is a passion and you're battling for an organization's survival or growth you should bring an entirely different perspective to your board interactions than if your end goal is to network and make connections. Although I personally feel you should act with character and within your beliefs no matter what your end goal, you may choose to take a less aggressive or different approach to certain matters depending on your reason for being on the board. That doesn't mean that you don't have an opinion—of course you'll have an opinion. But if your primary motivation in joining the board was to network and you find yourself in a disagreement with other board members, you might ask yourself if you truly need to go against the grain of the group in this particular instance. Attorneys often feel a need to argue and always be right, yet there is no need to always be right! This is especially true if asserting your opinion isn't advancing your end goal and is negatively impacting how others perceive you.

And as you remain conscious of your end goals, remember to let life pull you! You don't always need to try and make things happen. I'm not suggesting that you don't continue to take steps to meet your goals each day. You must definitely work on your plan and your goals in a consistent and committed manner. But do so mindfully! Just as you'll have days when things go extremely well, there will be days when things don't go as planned, days where you meet resistance at every turn. This resistance can be internal or external. When these experiences happen, step back and revise your daily plan when necessary. If you're consistent and mindful in approaching your goals, you'll achieve them. They may or may not be achieved in exactly the manner that you imagine, but they'll be achieved.

> LIFESTYLE TIP – *Establishing a daily yoga or meditation practice can help you learn how to reduce stress and anxiety, gain control over your mind, and develop healthier habits to relate and work better with others. It can also help you step back from situations that have not gone as expected and recalibrate how you are responding or perceiving these events. Being able to see the good in events or responding in a compassionate manner, can open doors and opportunities.*

To help you get to a mindful state, I'm going to ask you to find a way to be "selfishly mindful" every day. This could look like anything. Start your morning with meditation or yoga. Take the dog for a calm daily walk. Sit quietly while you drink a cup of coffee or tea or write for thirty minutes. The point is to establish a daily routine that gives you a few minutes to reflect and gather yourself so you can move through your life with intention, as the person that you want to be. For now, I would like you to think of just one thing you can do every day, one thing that brings you comfort and gives you a sense of calm. And then let this one thing become a place of refuge you can always return to, anchoring you in your best self, day after day.

I will be selfishly mindful each day by

_____

_____

BUILD YOUR "T"

Meeting your goals will likely depend on you distinguishing yourself in some way. One way to do this is to aim to become a "T-shaped lawyer." A T-shaped lawyer has deep expertise in one particular area of the law coupled with a broader capability across several other disciplines.[17] The T-shaped lawyer is slightly different than the traditional hybrid lawyer who has deep knowledge of the law and one other field—for example, an engineer/lawyer that becomes a successful patent lawyer or the nurse/lawyer that works for a pharmaceutical company or legal department in a hospital. A T-shaped lawyer has a deep understanding of their area of legal expertise (forming the base of the T) and a more varied knowledge across many disciplines (forming the top of the T).[18] The type of skills that make up the T can vary, but one would expect that some of the more sought-after T skills going forward will be in technology, eDiscovery technology, business, project management, data analytics, privacy and data security.

Changes in technology, the new legal market and new legal jobs have all combined to create demand for T-shaped lawyers in our modern legal era.[19] Because of their diverse and expansive knowledge base and the needs of our time, the T-shaped lawyer will likely become the mainstay of successful law firms in the next five to ten years. I challenge you to keep your eyes open for all classes, courses, certifications, and other opportunities that can add to your credentials and build your "T."

What interests or knowledge do I currently have that can be leveraged to help build my "T"?

_____

_____

_____

CONTINUE YOUR EDUCATION OUTSIDE OF LAW SCHOOL

Here are a few other ways to distinguish yourself and keep learning:

- Participate in webinars. On average, I take at least one to three free webinars a month. They keep me up-to-date and give me easy access to some of the most experienced attorneys in my industry. For me, this is a no brainer.

- Enroll in an EDI Distance Learning class. This is a great online learning program for eDiscovery attorneys. The $1 cost gives you access to numerous online webinars with attorneys that are working for Fortune 100 companies and AMLAW 100 law firms. This program is a great experience that offers you a deeper understanding of the eDiscovery industry and the expectations and stress points for in-house attorneys and outside counsel.

- Subscribe to free online publications that provide a quick glimpse into the hot legal topics of the day. Some you may want to check out include _LegalTech News,_ Law.com, ALM and _Corporate Counsel._

- Apply to be on a committee for your state bar association. Doing so is frequently free or inexpensive and will give you access to the attorneys and legal community in your local market. State bar associations also provide opportunities for local speaking engagements, publication, and continued learning.

- Write an article. Even if it doesn't get published or go viral, you're building confidence and gaining experience in the areas of your career and practice that most interest you. You are creating your voice. It'll pay off—maybe not in the way you initially expect, but in some way. If it doesn't get published, consider starting your own blog.

- Participate in live training through a mentorship program. Mentors provide customized one-on-one training and guidance. If you're interested in this invaluable experience, whether it's being a mentor or a mentee, you can often find a program through your law school or state bar association, or you can approach someone in your personal network to see if they would be willing to act in this capacity.

- Review the numerous online offerings or publications on specific areas of the law that will benefit your interests and career goals. There are many online publications, including publications by The Sedona Conference, that are excellent sources of information.

- Complete a certification course for a special technology platform. Many of the largest players in the technology field offer online and/or in-person training and certification. These certifications can be extremely useful in crafting your story or building your skills and might be the added expertise that sets you apart from other applicants.

- Develop a global mentality that includes, at least, a basic understanding of different cultures and laws. With the globalization of the world today, this type of basic understanding will be of growing importance. At a minimum, it'll be needed when advising or working for a global organization. Living abroad and traveling are two obvious ways to broaden your understanding of other cultures, but you can also learn more through reading other perspectives and meeting new people from different cultures.

Always be on the lookout for opportunities to expand your learning base and provide yourself with credentials in a variety of specialties, especially those related to technology. Smart companies are utilizing tech-savvy lawyers to implement and manage new technology in the legal department. The right technology training or certification can help you take advantage of these promising job opportunities, stay ahead of the curve and potentially become a leader in your field. Don't be blindsided by changes in the legal industry. Continue your education and get as much exposure as possible so that you can distinguish yourself as an expert!

WORK OVERSEAS

Another way to distinguish yourself is to work overseas. If this is something that interests you, I highly recommend considering options for working abroad. Not only will this help you develop a global mentality, but it'll also provide you with a valuable experience that immediately sets you apart from your peers. Once you have worked overseas, you can use this in your story and highlight the fact that you are in the minority of lawyers who've done this. Not many U.S. attorneys have worked abroad, and even fewer female attorneys have done so. This has become a compelling part of my story and can be a part of yours, too, if you choose to make it happen.

If you want to work oversees and you know what country you're interested in working in, consider contacting the Community Liaison Officer (CLO) at the embassy or consulate in that country to ask if they have local contacts looking to hire a U.S. attorney. Also, look at global law firms, global technology companies and LPOs to see if they have openings for U.S. attorneys abroad. For a good overview of potential resources see the FLO's Global Employment Initiative publication, Resources for

Lawyers Going Overseas.[20] The report provides a list of global legal recruiters, intergovernmental organizations (IGOs), nongovernmental organizations (NGOs), U.S. law firms with international offices and other groups that frequently have open positions for attorneys overseas. The report also offers tips and resources for starting your overseas job search.[21]

You may also find other paths that involve working abroad through the U.S. government. The State Department and Judge Advocate General's Corps (JAG) are two potential avenues that may appeal to you. The State Department has traditional attorney positions and less traditional attorney career paths, including positions as a foreign service officer, foreign service specialist, civil service, or career specialist. The State Department also offers student programs and professional fellowships.

LEVERAGE WHO YOU ARE: A FEMALE OR A MINORITY

Two well-respected judges, former Federal Judge Shira A. Scheindlin and Judge Jack B. Weinstein of the Federal District Court in Brooklyn, made headlines in 2017 for the part they both played in Judge Weinstein issuing a court rule that promotes and "creates an opportunity for a junior lawyer to participate."[22] Judge Weinstein's new rule was prompted by a report prepared by Judge Scheindlin that indicated in New York State trials and court hearings (across all levels of court and in all types of matters), male attorneys were still taking the lead about 75 percent of the time.[23]

It's a well-known fact that women and minorities are underrepresented in partnerships and in the court room. There are many different reasons for this imbalance and we won't go deeply into those questions or try to provide answers in this book. What we will discuss is how you can be involved in the groups, organizations, and movements that are available to assist women and minorities. While being a female, a minority, or both provides unique challenges in this industry, there are also resources that can help you leverage these aspects of who you are.

Where do you start? One way is to try and learn as much as you can about the culture of a potential employer before you even apply for a position. Consider reviewing reports on potential employers and law firms, like the one prepared by Working Mother Media, to get some insight into the culture of specific law firms and organizations. The list of Best Law Firms for Women prepared by Working Mother makes an annual selection of the law firms based on reports and surveys completed by current employees. The results include a brief profile of the selected firms, as well as the percentage of women partners and additional information on any attractive benefits that the firms offer.[24] Another resource is www.glassdoor.com, which is a job search tool that provides employee ratings, salary estimates, open job listings and much more.

You can also join one or more of the increasing number of women and minority organizations working to provide support to women and minorities in the legal industry. Groups like Women in eDiscovery (WiE), National Asian Pacific American Bar Association, Black Women Lawyers' Association of Greater Chicago (and other regional chapters), National Native American Bar Association and many others offer career advice, mentoring programs, business events and marketing assistance. These are excellent organizations that provide valuable resources. For example, the National Asian Pacific American Bar Association (NAPABA) has a national convention and regional conventions each year, both of which provide great networking opportunities as well as legal education on a wide variety of topics. The NAPABA has also started a monthly inspirational video series designed to bring about greater inclusion and understanding in America.[25] But please do not limit yourself to these resources. There are numerous organizations that can support you, so look for groups that align most closely with your interests, your location and your goals.

If you plan on starting your own company, there are programs available that provide financing or contracting opportunities for women and minorities. If your business meets the specified requirements, these programs can provide many benefits and opportunities.

In 1994, President Bill Clinton started the Women-Owned Small Business Federal Contracting Program, which set a goal to award 5 percent of U.S. government contracts to Women-Owned Small Businesses (WOSBs). When this goal was not reached as quickly as expected, Congress took another stab at lending support and on February 4, 2011, added the Small Business Association (SBA) rule, which identified 83 industries (this has now been expanded to include 113 industries) that were underrepresented by women.[26] The rule opened the door for more women in these industries to participate in federal contracting.[27]

In order for WOSBs to receive assistance, there are certain requirements that must be met, including that the business be certified as a small business and be U.S. women-owned and controlled.[28] Economically disadvantaged status can also be obtained in certain circumstances.[29] If these programs are of interest, additional information and assistance can be found at the U.S. Small Business Administration website, www.sba.gov.[30] Perhaps you can use one or more of these programs to help you meet your goals.

LIFESTYLE TIP – *Mentor a person you connect with or contribute to a group that interests you. If you're interested in biking, this might mean mentoring another female attorney that is also interested in biking. If you enjoy going to church, perhaps you could do volunteer work as an attorney for your church. The point is to build on those relationships that come naturally to you and that you enjoy. They'll be more authentic and rewarding. Remember this is the point of identifying the Lifestyle Lawyer in you—lifestyle benefits that are important to you. It'll help you identify your unique attributes and how best to share this part of you with the world.*

IDENTIFY THREE GROUPS THAT YOU CAN JOIN

Identify three groups that you can join to support you and your career goals. Then choose one to join today.

1. _____

2. _____

3. _____

7

NETWORK AND ESTABLISH YOURSELF AS AN EXPERT

Networking is one of the most important "unwritten rules" in business.[32] In a recent article by *Catalyst,* sixty-five men and women from various businesses were interviewed to determine what behaviors or actions were believed to play the most important role in developing or advancing their career opportunities. The number one response by a fairly significant amount was networking within and outside the organization. Connections were viewed as both a way to advance within the organization and a way to gain access to potential opportunities outside of your organization.

> *"It's not what you know, it's who you know!"*
>
> —*Paul Arden*[31]

Yet when I was in law school, networking was not emphasized nor was it all that important. You didn't need connections to be at the top of the class. But in the practice of law, your next business opportunity is more likely to come from a connection.

I know this was true for me. I was not at the very top of my law school graduating class. I was, however, one of the first people in my law school class to get an interview our senior year. I was also one of the first people to get a full-time job offer. Both of these opportunities were directly related to having "connections," people at the law firm where I was interviewing who I knew from law school and the community. I knew someone, they liked me, and that made them more comfortable with hiring me than an unknown entity (even an unknown entity with a higher GPA).

If networking doesn't come naturally to you, it may be hard to figure out where to start establishing new connections. There are so many ways to network—informal networks, formal business network events, mentoring programs, speaking engagements—and the options may feel overwhelming. This is where your prior work reflecting on your professional goals—where you've been, where you're going, where the legal market is headed, your strengths, your values, your vision—will be invaluable. This is also where the advice and assistance of a career counselor, a mentor, or a recruitment agent may be helpful. Once you're clear on who it is that you are and what it is that you want, it will be much easier to figure out what "professional community" you want to support. There are many legal organizations out there, and in this new age of technology they're all at your fingertips. Aligning yourself with the right group will open you up to new challenges to deepen your knowledge, develop connections, and expand your legal footprint. You may be surprised how many people are actually eager to help and share what they know.

Make sure that you're involved in the biggest or best organization possible, but also one that's a good fit for you and your personality. You may not be able to make the impact you want or need if the organization is too large. But that doesn't mean you shouldn't join the group; you should. You may just also need to join a smaller organization and build your experience speaking to a regional audience before you're ready to take the stage with the national organization. You may need to volunteer in a smaller group or subcommittee at the onset to get your feet wet, learn the dynamics of the organization and get noticed. Know yourself and others in the group. And don't forget networking can happen and connections can be made almost anywhere, during time spent enjoying hobbies, with church groups, while shopping or even on a plane.

When you're out there in your professional or semiprofessional networking scene, you'll be developing your professional image. Many will refer to this as your brand. Whether you refer to your professional image as your brand, or you call it something else, this is simply what people are saying about you when you leave the room—if they're talking at all. And you're most likely to be successful if they're talking and what they talk about are your strengths.

> *"Do Not Covet Your Ideas."*
>
> —*Paul Arden*[33]

One way to get people talking about you is to give away your ideas. Doing so will help build your reputation as, at the minimum, someone who has ideas in the first place, and hopefully as someone with good ideas they are willing to share. As you offer ideas, you're building your brand as a provider of solutions and information, and with such a brand, people will want to include you in the conversation, the solution, and the business. When you share your ideas publicly, you also receive valuable feedback. You can find out if people understand your idea and ask how you can make it better. Work with the group to refine and improve it—such an approach generally generates the most powerful ideas while also building relationships.

GET NOTICED AT YOUR CURRENT JOB

There are multiple ways to get noticed at your current job, which can greatly benefit your career whether or not you intend to stay in the position.

Do you have yearly reviews? If so, make sure you take advantage of these and are prepared to present a complete history of what you've accomplished, why these accomplishments are important, and how they added value to your firm or company. If you don't have yearly reviews, consider asking for a meeting to review your work. In addition to highlighting your accomplishments, also take the opportunity to ask for feedback regarding your performance and how you can improve.

Another way to get noticed in your current position is to build your client base and client relationships. When you want to build relationships with current and potential clients, one way is to make sure that you are listening to what the client has to say and helping them figure out what they need. If you don't fully understand their perspective, situation, or needs, ask more questions. And keep asking, until you get to the point that you truly understand. Remember the importance of listening actively and remaining engaged in the present moment. And if they aren't talking much, make sure you keep asking them questions to help them open up.

LIFESTYLE TIP – *Another advantage of working for a less traditional employer is you may have more access to some of the attorneys working for the world's top corporations and law firms. This can be a great lifestyle benefit to a job. It's potentially an excellent way to open doors and build connections that might lead to your next job. Young associates at law firms will generally not get these types of introductions and interactions with clients. See Chapter 11 for more information.*

This is not an area where everyone excels. In fact, I've seen C-suite level people that have spent valuable time and money to get in front of a client or potential client and what do they do? They just start talking and talk the entire time that has been allotted to them. While it's important to get your presentation, your goals, your vision, and what you're selling in front of the client or potential client, it's also important to use time together to ask them questions and learn more about their business needs. You may be at the presentation to sell them an eDiscovery solution when what they really need is a lawyer for an upcoming potential merger. If you've not taken the time to ask the potential client what it is they need, you may never find out and end up making the wrong sales pitch or miss the potential to provide new legal service solutions. By asking questions, you also start to connect. Clients and potential clients are much more likely to remember your name, your firm, or your company if they've had a real conversation with you and not just heard a presentation. They may even pick up the phone in a few weeks to discuss a new thought, problem, or project or share what is going on with the legal department. This type of relationship puts you one step closer to developing a partnership that will allow you to meet their needs in a superior way.

ASK QUESTIONS AND LISTEN ACTIVELY

Ask questions and listen actively to the answers wherever you go. I know it can be hard at times, but I challenge you to continually strive to do this better! Active listening will help you in your networking, goal-setting, mission-building, and personal life.

The next time you are in a conversation with someone (whether it is a personal conversation, a networking conversation, a business conversation, or an interview) stay keenly focused on asking and listening. Try to ask a follow-up question after each answer the other person gives that uses an element of their previous answer or what you just learned. I find that this process is much easier if I'm genuinely interested in the conversation. I've also found over the years of implementing this process that if I listen well, I can almost always find something I'm genuinely interested in talking and learning about. Frequently, if not always, you'll come away from this type of conversation with deeper knowledge of a person and often the realization that you have a common interest or goal. You now have a new connection: a potential client, a potential business partner, a potential referral source, or maybe a new friend.

PROFESSIONAL NETWORKING & COMMUNITY NETWORKING

Explore all different avenues for meeting people. Depending on your goals and the type of legal work you do, community programs that match your values may be the biggest return for the buck. If most of your business comes from your city, partic-ipating in a local church or exercise community may bring you more exposure than speaking at a national convention. Try out some different organizations and see what works best for you. Embrace the process, learn from it, and change it as needed while your career grows.

People are the driving force behind a successful business, so don't forget to attend company or law firm events and be a team player on a daily basis. Make sure that you support and appreciate your team. I hope this seems obvious to you, but many of my colleagues from my law firm days would frequently beg off and/or complain about attending firm events or retreats. If your company or law firm is spending the time and money to host an event, you need to be there and be present. If you aren't, people will notice.

Another great way to make great connections is to network with your competition. Pairing up with your competition may sound like a bad idea at first, but in all honesty, it's a good opportunity. Remember that not everyone is alike and not everyone connects in the same manner. On the surface, you may appear to be in competition but if you look at each other closely, you may find that your personalities and the type of customers you would attract are different. Maybe not completely different but slightly different, in a way you can use to your advantage. And even if one person is "stronger" than the other, that doesn't mean that there won't still be room to share potential clients, referrals, or ideas. Additionally, their "competing" firm or company may also be looking to hire someone one day.

As you meet people in a variety of settings, always give everyone an opportunity to talk. Asking questions is the easiest way to break the silence and make a connection. People generally like to talk about themselves and find it easy and comforting to answer specific questions. You can keep it simple. For example, you can ask:

- What do you like to do on the weekends?

- How long have you been an attorney?

- What is your favorite restaurant?

There aren't too many wrong questions.

Tell them a little about yourself as well, but make sure that you don't spend too long on this. And if the opportunity presents itself, make sure that you introduce your new connection to other people, adding in some of the information your new connection has just shared with you. This helps establish the relationship. Finally, before you wrap up the conversation, see if they'd like to set up a meeting for the following week to talk more.

LIFESTYLE TIP – *If you're constantly going to events that are full of attorneys, consider going to an event where there aren't many attorneys. And as hard as it is to believe, they do exist—we just aren't accustomed to going to them. You'll likely meet new people with new ideas. You'll also probably find it refreshing to talk to people that aren't accustomed to mingling with attorneys. At the very least, you can work on refining your networking skills.*

KNOW HOW TO TELL YOUR STORY

Listening to others and not constantly putting the spotlight on yourself is an important part of networking. There will be many times, though, when you should share your own story—including times when you're keeping the focus on others. An effective personal story should fit into one sentence that can leave a strong impression of who you are, one that will remain long after you've stopped talking about yourself.

We've talked about building this story. Now it's time to refine and shape your story, keep the following in mind:

- Make sure you've taken the time to define who you are in your life and career and how you got there.

- Think about what it is you do to help make situations in the office or world better.

- Try to identify whether there's an emotional element to your story you can use to engage people and help them connect with you.

- Make sure your story is consistent, memorable and easy to understand.

- Know your market, who your competition is and how you're different from your competitors.

- Prepare one sentence that makes people understand who you are and how you are different.[34]

SELF-PROMOTION/BRANDING

Self-promotion and branding can help you make the important connections that will further your career and improve your professional standing.

In their book, *Branding Yourself: How to Use Social Media to Invent or Reinvent Yourself*, Erik Deckers and Kyle Lacy write, "Branding yourself means that you create the right kind of emotional response you want people to have when they hear your name, see you online, or meet you in real life."[35] But always remember that to have an effective brand, it needs to capture your authentic self and at the same time fit your industry; and if you want to do this, you'll need to be projecting real competency and success, whatever success looks like to you. Remember that the best way to succeed in business and your personal life is to be kind to other people and add real value to their lives. Also remember that you can be as good as you want to be. You may need more practice to catch up with the people in your industry that you admire, but you can do it with the right approach and work ethic. It also helps immensely to be passionate about what you're doing. This is a hard one to fake, so if you aren't passionate about what you do, I would suggest you find the thing you're passionate about and do that instead.

Promoting yourself and your unique self, your authentic self, will take work. But you can do it. Even simple steps such as introducing yourself to the organizer of a conference and telling him or her you're interested in speaking at a future event can open new doors for your career. If this type of self-promotion feels frightening, try to shift your mindset. For example, instead of thinking about what you're asking someone to do for you, like give you an opportunity to speak at a big conference, think about the message you want to share with people while speaking. Think about what it is that you're offering. Female lawyers need to learn not only how to sell themselves, but that it's okay to do so.

LIFESTYLE TIP – *If self-promotion feels frightening, try to shift your mindset. Remember negative brain chatter is bad. Instead of thinking, "I'm dreading asking my boss to put me on this case, he might not think I'm ready to handle this project," try this on for size: "I really am passionate about the new case we just got in the office. I could make a difference in the outcome of this case. You know, 'XXX roofing' is a great company—I would love to be part of the trial team." See how different that sounds? You aren't asking for a favor, you're giving your boss, and the firm's client, something valuable. An attorney that's passionate about a case and wants to make a difference in the outcome. Think about what it is that you're offering. Female lawyers need to learn not only how to sell themselves, but that it's okay to do so. You and your services are helping people be more efficient, successful, and safe. If you don't get put on the case, you've at least let people know that you believe you're capable of taking on this type of work. This will likely help you land the next big project or case.*

USE TECHNOLOGY: FOR NETWORKING, BRANDING & SELF-PROMOTION

Technology offers a variety of opportunities to network and promote yourself, your brand, and your business. Here are some ways you can get started using today's tools to advance your career:

- Use social media daily in a way that aligns with and builds your professional identity.

- Consider hiring professional help to create an amazing website.

- Find your specialty—your niche—and write articles about it, blog about it, tweet about it . . . just get it, and yourself, out there for people to see.

- Leverage your writing to get speaking engagements with organizations, conferences, or local bar associations.

- Highlight what is different or special about yourself, your company, or your firm.

You should always be thinking of how to use technology for networking, branding & self-promotion. Is Facebook, LinkedIn, Twitter, or the next big thing to promote yourself the best route to take? Be on the lookout for how other attorneys in your field/industry are networking. However, it's important to be careful of potential ethical issues for lawyers and law firms. A small part of what has kept the legal industry from embracing change has been the ethical canons and requirements surrounding the practice of law.

Here is one example of the ethical complications attorneys can face. In June of 2017, the New Jersey Supreme Court issued an opinion that lawyers in New Jersey "may not participate in the Avvo legal service programs because the programs improperly require the lawyer to share a legal fee with a non-lawyer in violation of Rule of Professional Conduct 5.4 (a), and pay an impermissible referral fee in violation of Rule of Professional Conduct 7.2 (c) and 7.3 (d)." Avvo, LegalZoom, and Rocket Lawyer were all cited by the New Jersey State Bar Association, which issued a specific inquiry into whether nonlawyer-owned online services were permissible and ethical. LegalZoom's and Rocket Lawyer's models were found to be permissible while Avvo's arrangement was found to be in violation, as the fees were determined an "impermissible referral fee." As millennials become the core of the workforce and technology continues to advance, we may eventually see some changes in the Rules of Professional Conduct for Lawyers, but until then be careful as you tread into new waters. Always make sure you're in compliance with the rules.

TELL YOUR STORY IN ONE SENTENCE

What do you do? _____

_____

_____

_____

How do you make situations in the office or world better?

_____

_____

_____

_____

Is there an emotional element to your story you can use to engage people and help them connect with you? _____

_____

_____

_____

Prepare one sentence that makes people understand who you are and how you are different from your competition.

_____

_____

_____

_____

At this point, you should have a strong sense of your story, your vision, your strengths, your needs, and the emerging opportunities in our new legal world. Now it's time to move to the next step. Let's begin to take a detailed look at the six legal career paths and some of the lifestyle benefits of each so you can determine what path can help you build the life you're currently dreaming about.

SECTION 2

Six Lawyer Paths & Their Lifestyle Benefits

8

THE LAW FIRM PATH

Similar to the belief that many women have been taught they have to be thin to be beautiful, many female lawyers have learned the only way to be a happy and successful lawyer is to be a partner at the top law firm. Why is that? Law firm jobs frequently come at the expense of taking time away from our families and from the activities we enjoy. Does the image of the perfect law firm practice come from television shows or John Grisham books? Whatever the source, it continues to be the number one choice for law school graduates. According to the ABA 2016 Law Graduate Employment Data Report, 44.1 percent of all law school graduates took positions with law firms.[36] By comparison, the runner-up position was with "business and industry" and accounted for only 13.5 percent of law school graduates.[37]

It's true there are many advantages to a career with a traditional law firm. You get to say, "I did it!" And after you land the coveted job, you put in the hours and you end up getting valuable experience. Firms really can be a great place to learn how to practice law—to begin to learn what they don't teach in law school. Being with a big firm also gives you access to support and resources which help you get started specializing in a certain area of the law. And typically, law firms provide a comfortable salary and good benefits. So there are definitely some good reasons to take the traditional law firm path when you graduate.

While this may be a valid dream and goal for some women, it's not the only option nor is it the only path to success. Many female attorneys will, in fact, have as much if not more success if they have a less stressful job, one giving them more time to spend with their families, or simply some free time to travel outside of work. Identifying and accepting what a "successful career" means to you is part of the challenge and point of being a Lifestyle Lawyer. There are also disadvantages to the traditional law firm practice. And realizing the challenges of working for a traditional law firm and the challenges these firms are now facing is a necessary step in determining whether this coveted path is a good fit for you.

THE TRADITIONAL LAW FIRM PRACTICE TODAY

Attorney Scale: 90%–100% legal focus

Pay: These are prestigious jobs providing a platform to build your career, potentially become a partner and make a good salary with excellent benefits. According to Robert Half 2017 Salary Guide, lawyers with over ten years of experience working in a large law firm can expect an average salary range of $209,500 to $288,250. For lawyers with over ten years of experience, at a small or mid-size law firm, you can expect an average salary range of between $122,000 to $270,500. Comparatively, if you have four to nine years of experience, you can expect to make between $86,500 to $234,500, depending on the size of the firm.[38]

Getting started: There is a lot of competition for these jobs, so it can be difficult to get in the door.

Once you have the job: Expect long work hours, stressful work and billable hour requirements.

Flexibility: Don't expect much flexibility. You may be able to work from home in some instances, but you will likely need to be working long hours wherever you are.

Watch out for: Dead-end firms that are losing clients and are not prepared for the new legal market.

Lifestyle Benefit: This is the Cadillac of career paths. For attorneys interested in climbing the traditional career ladder, prestige, or a big salary, the traditional law firm will generally continue to be the best route.

I have worked with and interviewed many female lawyers, and throughout these conversations the most frequently referenced disadvantage to working for a big firm is the billable hour requirement and the work-life balance. This is not to say that female attorneys can't have a successful career at a law firm and ultimately rise to be a partner. They can! But there is a trade-off for the female attorney that takes the law-firm partnership career path. If you are already on this path and it's working for you, then you're fortunate to have found a good firm that provides the right support and partnership track for your career.

Female attorneys are being conditioned to believe that we have to tough it out, that we can have it all. But sometimes sticking it out may not the best choice and will end up with the opposite result. As we all know too well many female attorneys end up dropping out of the workforce completely, particularly when they are on the law-firm partnership track. So always remember, what is right for you might not mean being partner at a law firm and raising three children and two dogs. It may instead mean making the difficult decision to leave your law firm and find a new career that allows you to work from home, or only work four days a week, or has some other advantage that meets your goals and needs as a female and as a female lawyer.

I will be forever thankful to Leitner, Williams, Dooley & Napolitan for the support the firm provided in my development as an attorney. But even with that support, there came a time in my career when I no longer felt I could continue to bill the hours and meet the demands of my clients and partnership while raising my children. This was a choice I made personally and there are plenty of women that have made the opposite choice and made it work. However, if you ever contemplate leaving your practice, I can assure you that you are not alone. Most women working full-time and having children will contemplate how best to proceed with their careers at some point. But if you do decide to leave your law firm or the practice of law, it's important to make sure that you position yourself where you can return if you later decide to do so.

So, with that in mind, let's look at the legal landscape and challenges for the law firm today so you can determine whether you want to embark on or remain on this path, and if you're on it, how to thrive.

We're first going to step back a few years to 2006 and 2007, when the mortgage crisis hit the U.S. and ultimately resulted in the 2008 global financial crisis. According to the Center for the Study of the Legal Profession at the Georgetown University Law Center, "The global economic meltdown brought to an abrupt end a long period of unprecedented prosperity for law firms— more than a decade of almost uninterrupted growth in demand, revenues, and profits."[39]

Gone are the days when the corporate counsel automatically picked up the phone and sent all projects to an outside law firm. There will still be times when this happens, but increasingly the corporate legal department will first look at the costs involved in sending the project out to the law firm and whether it is necessary or if there is another more efficient way to accomplish the same task.

How has this affected the traditional law firm model? Traditional law firms are feeling the effects of changes being made by corporations and many are starting to adjust their business models in response. One of the main challenges facing law firms today is determining how the firm can continue to maintain their client base and still make money.

Big firms are also feeling the effects of changes in technology and the disruption of the legal market, even if they aren't acutely aware of the disruption upon them. According to the 2017

Altman Weil Survey, "there are few law firm leaders who would dispute the permanency of more price competition, a need for greater efficiency, an influx of new kinds of competitors, and the inexorable force of technology innovation."[40] If firms are truly making changes to get ahead of technology trends, or at least, stay in step with the changes in technology, then they'll likely be met with excited and eager clients. The legal revolution will reward attorneys and the law firms that are able to bring technology and innovation together to provide more effective, efficient, and value-driven services to clients.

However, significant change in the traditional law firm environment isn't coming easily or quickly. Perhaps senior lawyers close to retirement figure that in a few more years they'll be gone and the firm is doing "good enough" to get by until they are gone? Or maybe they just don't know how to sufficiently change their delivery model? If you're on a traditional law-firm partnership path you may already be aware of these issues. Whether it's happening at your own firm, or to friends and colleagues, we have all heard stories about there not being enough work. If you're looking to work for a law firm or transition to a new law firm, ask questions regarding whether the firm is taking appropriate steps to keep up with the changes in technology and adopting forward-thinking business models to meet client expectations.

What might these steps look like? Two of the most promising things a traditional law firm can do is come up with true alternative pricing models and embrace new delivery models that include technology and innovative partnerships to provide more efficient services. Firms that are embracing technology by bringing on AI legal research tools, adopting in-house technology solutions, innovating new service delivery models or outsourcing to Alternative Legal Service Providers (ALSPs) as cost-cutting measures for the firm and their clients will likely be the leaders in the coming decade.

There are other ways firms can take advantage of technology to improve their business. DLA Piper reported at ILTACON in 2017 that they'd used "predictive analytics" based on client metrics to help figure out which clients were staying and why they were staying. The director of sector marketing at DLA Piper, Kim Rennick, looked at historical data to analyze why some client's business was growing in comparison to other clients that were sending less work to the firm. After the results were in, DLA Piper was able to take a closer look at certain variables that they determined were important in the law firm/client relationship. The end result was that DLA Piper reported the prevention of an 85 percent fee loss on a yearly basis with an estimated increase in revenue of $37.6 million.[41] This is one unique way to use technology to help your firm get ahead.

WHAT TO EXPECT WHILE WORKING IN A TRADITIONAL LAW FIRM ENVIRONMENT

Most attorneys practicing in a law firm will develop a core practice area in one, possibly two, areas of practice. You'll also be billing every six minutes of every business day, unless you're with a more innovative firm that's developing alternative billing models, but you'll also likely have more autonomy over your day-to-day life. You'll be in charge of your own calendar and setting your own schedule. You'll be seen as an attorney and, for the most part, an equal in the law firm environment. You'll have a certain amount of job security and a clearly defined career path.

As we all know, you may encounter a bias in favor of men in the big firm environment. A substantial portion of female attorneys I interviewed felt that their firm favored male attorneys over female attorneys and believed the office policies and rules were more beneficial for the male associates. Women frequently complained about the stress of meeting billable hour requirements. These problems often increased as females were looking to have children, the timing of which frequently coincided with being up for a partnership position. This created a stressful environment for both the women associates and the partners in the firm.

Many of the female attorneys that I interviewed had at some point in their career left the traditional law firm job and continued working as an attorney at another firm or in another legal career altogether. While this transition to other jobs was a success for some, many of them returned to their positions at the original law firm after a short time period. This type of turnover and return to the same job happens more frequently than you might expect.

I've seen this happen several times with attorneys that I've worked with. Trying to understand this phenomenon is important for several reasons. First, if you're unhappy in your current position and want to explore an alternative career, it's always best that you give your employer enough notice of your intent to leave and that you leave on the best terms possible. You never know if you'll want or need to return to your former position. It's also the best way to conduct yourself and will improve your image as a person and an attorney throughout the legal community. Second, many attorneys realized the office environment was not as difficult, or different from other jobs, as they'd once thought. For many lawyers, their first real entry into the job world will be as a first-year associate at a law firm. They've had limited experience working full-time. It may take leaving a firm and working at another law office to realize that there is a business component to running a law firm. Some business decisions are made to keep the business going and profitable. However, it may also be true that the specific law firm that you're working for may not be the best fit for you. If that's the case, then making a move to another firm or type of practice may be an excellent solution.

In the alternative, you may learn that working at a law firm is not for you. And knowing that is invaluable and will likely make you happier and more focused on success in your next job.

HYBRID LAW FIRMS

Some law firms have started to try and increase efficiency and profitability by using a variety of new staffing models, including setting up departments within the firm that are staffed by contract or part-time attorneys in an effort to control costs, increase profit margins and meet client demands. This is creating a new hybrid law firm. One part of the firm is built around the more traditional law firm model that allows associates to enter into the practice with a goal of advancing to a partner level one day, while another part of the firm incorporates new attorney tracks for associates that aren't on the traditional partnership path.

This hybrid model is advantageous in several ways. It creates a new income line for the law firm that is frequently more profitable to their bottom line. It also provides a needed service to clients that want to get more for less; it allows the firm to have a subcategory of lawyers or a separate division that's more focused on repetitive tasks that can help lower costs and provide a better final product; and it lets the firm offer a culture potentially attractive to less traditional lawyers, younger lawyers and female lawyers. These positions generally pay a little less and do not promise a partner position at the end of the rainbow. They do, however, offer more flexible working environments that may encourage out-of-state positions, at-home work, and other flexible work solutions. This type of working environment may benefit an attorney that's not set on making partner but still wants to work in big law.

Attorney Scale: 80% to 90% legal focus & 10% to 20% technology focus

Pay: The pay at these jobs will be attractive for entry-level attorneys and depending on the area of the country you live in, you could still make more money working remotely for a big firm in a hybrid law position than working as an attorney in a traditional firm in your hometown. In general, though, you can expect to make less than at a traditional law firm in the same region of the country.

Getting started: These jobs are still competitive, but less competitive then landing a traditional law firm job. Frequently, you'll find a very narrow and defined type of legal work being performed.

Once you have the job: Keep your options open for ways to use any specialized skills you're developing and pursue continuing education in case you want to transition to a different career in the future.

Lifestyle Benefit – Flexibility: These jobs typically provide more flexibility in your work-life balance. You may be able to work remotely, part-time, or on a project basis. These issues are important to lifestyle lawyers.

Watch out for: Keep your expectations in check; you're not on a partnership track.

Lifestyle Benefit – Vision compatibility: These jobs will be better suited for attorneys that value flexibility and work-life balance most. If climbing the career ladder or a big salary is important to you, this isn't the best route.

LEGAL JOBS IN LAW FIRMS FOCUSED ON TECHNOLOGY AND PROJECT MANAGEMENT

As mentioned above, cutting-edge firms are also implementing new technology solutions that require project management positions. These positions are frequently filled by attorneys, or in some instances senior paralegals that also have technology skills. These firms are being rewarded as they provide corporate clients with the innovation and value they need while maintaining a high level of service and security over confidential client information. Having attorneys on staff that can manage the growing vendor relationships for clients is a significant component for a successful delivery model. These new positions are focused on keeping the project on track and establishing defensible delivering models that also meet costs and court-ordered delivery timelines. With these new business models, perhaps the "old-school" law firm can find a way to thrive in the new age of law. Here are what a couple of these new positions look like:

Legal Project Manager: A person in this role will help keep the project on track and ensure delivery within costs and at appropriate standards. This position requires good interpersonal skills and time management, as well as the ability to lead teams. Since project management skills will be helpful in this position, a certification in project management may help you land the job. See www.pmi.org, www.iapp.org and other similar sites for online courses and certification in project management.

Legal Technologist: These are a new breed of data geeks that can bridge the gap between law and technology. A person in this position works with the predictive analytics needed to make best use of Big Data and helps law firms make strategic decisions. A technology background will frequently be required to fill this position.

Attorney Scale: 50% legal focus & 50% technology/project management focus

Quality & Pay: These jobs will provide you with a platform to build your career and make a good salary with excellent benefits.

Getting started: There will be competition for these jobs at the most prestigious firms, but having the right balance of a good legal pedigree and the extra skills needed for these developing positions may set you apart from others applying.

Once you have the job: Keep your options open for ways to use the specialized skills you're developing and keep up your legal skills and education in case you want to transition to a different career in the future.

Flexibility: Most of these jobs in big law firms will likely require fairly regular work hours, with a certain amount of autonomy to work away from the office on a limited basis.

Watch out for: Pigeonholing yourself into a very narrow area of practice that may limit your ability to move into other legal career paths in the future. With the right technology training and networking, you might be able to open more career doors outside of the legal industry.

Lifestyle Benefit – Vision compatibility: This job is well suited to the attorney who wants to be able to leave the job at the office. You can expect to have a fairly manageable career that will not keep you up at night.

TRUE STORIES OF WOMEN ON THE LAW FIRM PATH

I was asked to speak at the 2018 Women's Empowerment Conference in Nashville, Tennessee. It was a great event and I met some spectacular women attorneys of all ages and from all types of legal backgrounds. As you might suspect, many of the women who attended have spent most of their careers practicing law in a mostly "white male" lawyer's world. But in spite of the challenges, or possibly in some cases *because* of the challenges, we had a room full of female attorneys who are all still practicing law and who want to help make the profession better and more hospitable for all women. I left the conference with this question: why had these women stayed in the profession, when so many other female attorneys had left?

Statistically, there are more women graduating from law school than men. But according to a survey by the American Bar Association in 2017, 64% of practicing attorneys are male— only 36% are female.[42]

Is it because they got lucky and found the perfect legal job the first time? Although that may be the case in some instances, it isn't the real answer to what keeps women attorneys working. Some female attorneys have stayed in the work force even when they weren't happy in their job. They continued to look for the perfect job—even when they didn't have to.

One female partner who I've known and worked with for years (I'll call her Ruth) is the type of person who is always on the go, has multiple projects and responsibilities at home and work, and is always willing to stop and help a friend. Having graduated from law school in the mid-1990s, her first career options were more limited than they are today. Not surprisingly, she took the traditional law firm path and was very successful in her practice—both as an attorney and as a rainmaker for the firm. She made partner in six years at a time when there were only three female partners in a firm of approximately 125 attorneys. On the surface, everything was perfect.

But Ruth had been unhappy and stressed with the partners for years, though few looking in from the outside would have realized it. She was also bringing that stress home after work. After more than a decade, she finally made the difficult choice to leave her partnership, and transitioned to another firm. Many people, myself included, did not expect Ruth's move to a different firm to fix the problem. Yet when I followed up with her several years later, she told me that her transition had relieved most of the stress and unhappiness she felt at her former firm. She said she couldn't be happier with her decision to leave her old firm and start anew.

While changing your firm may not always result in a better situation, we all know that sometimes a change is needed to renew our spirits, minds and attitudes. If your current work situation isn't working for you, it's up to you to take the time to figure out the cause and then take steps to change things. And sometimes, a move to a new space will change your mindset and make all the difference in the world. It's possible that Ruth's new satisfaction in her new firm had at least as much to do with her different mindset as with different work conditions.

But why had Ruth persevered with her law career at all? What led her to continue pushing, looking for another firm that would be a better fit? Many women would likely have left the field entirely. When Ruth was making this decision to keep searching for the right firm, she had two small children and a loving husband with a good job; she didn't have to keep being a lawyer to pay the bills. What was her motivation?

What most people (male or female) want is to have meaningful lives where they're contributing and making a difference. Each of us has our own unique qualities and gifts that we bring to the table. We also have our own past experiences and values that make up the core of who we are. All of these experiences together direct our efforts and guide us in our daily lives, whether we're aware of this or not. Ruth has a strong need to work. As I've talked to her over the years, I get the feeling that her drive stems from a close relationship with her father and the beliefs and goals he instilled in her from a young age. Whether this was a conscious decision or not, Ruth has definitely followed her instinct that, in order to be her happiest, most well-rounded self, she needs to work!

We can all find examples and mentors like Ruth who inspire us to keep looking for ways to make our careers work, whether it's someone we know personally or someone we only read about. Marianne Short has made it big as managing partner at a top law firm and General Counsel. After graduating from Boston College Law School in 1976, she served briefly as the Special Assistant Attorney General for the State of Minnesota before joining Dorsey & Whitney LLP in 1977.[43] Short was a litigator for 30 years and became the managing partner at Dorsey in 2007. She held that position for five years, until 2012, when she became the Chief Legal Officer and Executive Vice President of UnitedHealth Group on January 1, 2013. In 2017, *Corporate Counsel Magazine* listed Short as the fifth-highest-paid General Counsel in the country, with reported annual earnings of $2,598,100.[44] She's a great example of a female attorney who has broken the glass ceiling and excelled in two female lawyer career paths.

FINANCIAL IMPLICATIONS OF GOING WITH A FIRM

There are financial advantages to going with a law firm job. Working at a top-tier law firm, or regional law firm, can be the most certain way for most attorneys to make a good salary and benefits. It's also likely to provide more long-term career stability if you're aligned with the right law firm and eventually make partner. However, if this career path isn't well suited for your talents and life it may end up forcing you out of the practice of law entirely. Thus having a negative effect on your finances if you look at the whole of your career.

HOW TO TRANSITION TO THE LAW FIRM PATH

If you're interested in the law firm path, carefully consider how you might navigate this transition. Keep in mind the following actions you'll need to take and questions you'll need to answer:

- You need to have a plan. This plan needs to be in writing and it needs to be a living plan that grows as you mature as an attorney. You should also look into résumé preparation, interview preparation, additional online education or certification, and possibly even career coaching before you pursue that coveted job.

- Know your competition. Know what's going on in the industry and what type of law firm you want to work for.

- Once you've identified a firm you want to work for, answer these crucial questions:

  - How is the firm anticipating that its work structure or workflow in the coming one to five years will change? How will that impact your potential role with the firm?

  - Is the law firm business model that is in place working and sustainable for the next twenty years?

  - If you are looking to go on a traditional partnership track, does the firm still offer a partnership track? If so, what will you be inheriting?

- Know your strengths and weaknesses. Always be on the lookout to improve on your strengths and limit your weaknesses. Take some time to make sure that you are prepared and qualified for the job and the firm where you are looking to work.

9

THE CORPORATE PATH

T he second-most favored path for attorneys to take is a job with a company as an in-house attorney. For many female attorneys, the belief has been that taking a job at a corporation allows for a 9-to-5 work schedule and the ability to, in essence, have their cake and eat it too. But is that still the case? Is the in-house position still the coveted choice for female attorneys?

For some, going in-house is still an excellent career choice. But with changes in the global economy, the legal environment, and technology, the in-house role has changed significantly over the past ten to fifteen years. Businesses and their legal departments have seen increased pressures—to provide more services at reduced costs without increasing the head count of the legal department. These factors are putting pressure on in-house counsel and legal departments to think "outside the box" to meet corporate demands. Changes in technology and the globalization of our business world have also created a vast array of new laws, regulations, and challenges that are affecting businesses in the U.S. and around the world, and as technology advances and our economy becomes increasingly global, change will continue. Here is a closer look at some of the current tasks and challenges that in-house legal departments are facing, the changes that they are undergoing and the effects these changes are having on the daily life of corporate attorneys.

WHAT TO EXPECT WHEN YOU GO TO WORK IN-HOUSE

Attorney Scale: 70% legal focus & 30% business focus

Pay: These are prestigious jobs that'll provide you with a decent salary to start and the opportunity to make a very good salary with excellent benefits as your career progresses.

The Robert Half Salary Guide for 2018 reports an average salary range of $128,750 to $306,000 for a general counsel. In-house counsel with over ten years of experience can expect to make between $114,500 to $255,750. In-house counsel with less than nine years of experience will average between $63,500 to $190,750.[45]

Getting started: There's a lot of competition for these jobs, so it can be difficult to land your first position. This is especially true if you're coming straight out of law school.

Once you have the job: Expect structured office hours and having to balance a large volume of work across many areas of expertise.

Flexibility: Some companies are starting to offer more flexibility and alternative lifestyle benefits to retain talent.[46] You may be able to work from home in some instances, but you'll likely be working long hours whether at home or the office. In 2017, 23 percent of respondents indicated that the most important reason that they went to work in their current position was the lifestyle benefit of a flexible work day.[47]

Watch out for: The career expectancy at a corporation is less than at a law firm. Due to business pressures, corporate reorganization, and hiring of new CEOs and general counsel, it's unlikely that you will start and finish your career at the same company.

Lifestyle Benefit – Vision compatibility: This is an excellent career path for attorneys with an inclination toward business. Were you considering an MBA when you went to law school? If you're interested in developing a wide variety of legal skills, making a good salary, and having the potential to advance your career, this might be your route. According to a survey from Special Counsel's Parker + Lynch, 23 percent of the 500 legal professionals reported that opportunity for growth, along with the previously mentioned flexible work arrangements, was the most important reason that they took their current position.[48] Other significant draws for going in-house included co-workers, compensation, and working for a company that's making a difference in the world.[49] It's also a good option for the attorney that's interested in having some time and energy left over for their family and personal life at the end of the day. If you're a technology-savvy, business-minded lawyer who likes to think on your feet and works well with others, this may be the perfect job for you. There may be options to distinguish yourself from the rest of the in-house legal team by becoming a subject matter expert. Ways to establish yourself include speaking at conferences or publishing articles. Also, consider whether an international corporation is an attractive fit for your personality. The bigger the corporation, the smaller role and authority you're likely to have as an attorney. Smaller corporations are more likely to offer a bigger role for attorneys, with less structure and clarity around your job duties.

HOW BEING IN-HOUSE MAY BE DIFFERENT FROM A LAW FIRM PRACTICE

Working in-house will require you to develop the skills to handle a broad range of disciplines. While the attorney practicing with a large law firm will likely become a specialist in some area of the law, the attorney that enters an in-house position will be less likely to have the opportunity to specialize in any particular discipline. From a practical standpoint, this means the in-house attorney will have to be comfortable with not always being the expert in the room and with frequently being required to make decisions with the limited information available during a crisis.

One aspect of being in-house that many attorneys enjoy is learning about the business and being a part of the business. Understanding what the company does or sells is a necessary part of becoming a valuable member of the in-house legal team. Some companies even require that their corporate legal team spend time working in their stores or with the products that they sell, to give them exposure to the challenges the employees face on a daily basis and help them understand how the business works from the ground up.

As a corporate attorney, you won't have to bill every six minutes of every business day. You'll be freed from the billable hour. The trade-off, though, is that you'll likely have less autonomy over your day-to-day life. Whereas you're frequently free to set your own schedule in the law firm, that isn't always the case for a corporate attorney that will be asked to follow corporate guidelines, policies and procedures. You may also find that the practice of law in-house is very different than in a law firm. For example, the hierarchical nature of the company structure is usually much different than the law firm where you're seen as an attorney, either an associate or a partner, but an attorney. This hierarchy also has implications for a general counsel that is reporting to the board and the CEO of the company. In the book *The Generalist Counsel* by Prashant Dubey and Eva Kripalani, you can find a detailed explanation of the benefits and disadvantages for attorneys that are considering the in-house career path. [50] I highly recommend this book to attorneys that are considering the move and want to get some additional insight from several prominent in-house attorneys that have transitioned from law firms to become general counsel at large U.S. companies.

The General Counsel (GC) is tasked with overseeing the legal affairs for all departments of the business. Today this includes handling ongoing litigation and legal issues, as well as overseeing and identifying potential legal issues or risks across the company. The role of the GC has grown beyond what we once thought of as a traditional in-house legal role; it's evolved in many companies to a position that also helps develop and oversee strategies to keep the business growing and on the right track. As part of the general counsel's team:

- You'll be tasked with handling a larger variety of work in-house. Whereas once the in-house legal department would send almost all interesting and important work to their outside counsel, today the in-house team will frequently keep a much larger portion of this work while still sending the more complex legal work to specialized outside counsel at law firms. The in-house team will also handle some portion of legal proceedings and administrative tasks internally.

- Your role will often include increasing legal awareness across the organization, introducing standard operating procedures, risk management, compliance reporting, public policy advocacy, mergers and acquisitions, labor law, litigation, eDiscovery, intellectual property, and advising on cybersecurity issues.

- You're a part of the business and will work across all business departments. As in-house counsel, you'll be faced with ongoing daily questions from all business departments regarding legal concerns. Another part of your job will be to manage risks and potential risks across all departments.

HOW TECHNOLOGY IS BEING USED IN THE LEGAL DEPARTMENT

Technology is making projects smarter and more efficient. Corporations are constantly expecting more for less, and this creates opportunities for attorneys that are willing and able to do things differently. If you can bring new business ideas and solutions to the job with a combination of a legal background and the technology knowledge to make things happen, you'll have the tools to excel in the in-house legal department. Technology is being brought in-house to help increase efficiency, provide a better product and save money. According to Zapproved's 2017 survey, there has already been a significant increase in corporate use of automated legal hold technology: 34 percent of legal departments in 2013 and 57 percent of legal departments in 2017 are reporting that they're using automation software to initiate legal holds.[51] Part of the increase in use of technology is based on the continuing decrease in the cost and another part is based on the confidence the technology brings to the defensibility of processes.

As technology continues to advance, it'll become more mainstream in corporate America. In-house legal teams will need attorneys that understand that these changes are coming, see their benefits, and know how to implement the changes with minimal disruption to the legal department.

LIFESTYLE LAWYERS THAT ARE CYBERSECURITY EXPERTS

Companies, regulators, and customers are increasingly concerned about data protection. In 2017, we saw an uptick in reports of companies being hacked and millions of customers having their personal data compromised, which brought negative attention to companies and put increased pressure on the IT and legal departments. Being prepared to deal with potential and ongoing cybersecurity challenges and ensuring data privacy and information security concerns are addressed is going to continue to be an important component of in-house legal work.

Today there is a growing relationship between the legal department and the IT department. The legal director continues to be tasked with drafting, implementing, and ensuring employee compliance with legal data protection policies for the company. Data protection policies must be in place for clients, suppliers, and the company's own employees. The legal department may also be tasked with educating employees across the organization to make sure they're aware of and following data protection rules and policies. The cost for protecting personal data continues to be on the rise. Some studies estimate that as much as $86.4 billion will be spent on information security in 2017.[52] With this type of media attention and money on the table, we can expect to see in-house legal departments looking to hire lawyers that have experience in cybersecurity and privacy protection.

LIFESTYLE LAWYERS THAT ARE SUBJECT MATTER EXPERTS IN EDISCOVERY

In the eDiscovery field in-house legal teams must be prepared to deal with ongoing eDiscovery challenges. Due to growing volumes of data and voluminous eDiscovery requests, companies are no longer automatically sending the review work to the outside counsel that is handling the litigation. Companies have increasingly been sending document review work to either onshore or offshore review teams to save money. Onshore teams of U.S. attorneys will typically work in a lower-cost district of the country, like Florida, Michigan or Kansas. "Offshore" vendors are located in another country, frequently India or the Philippines. This type of multi-lawyer review allows your in-house attorney team or outside counsel to place lower-cost resources on the initial review of documents. The second-phase review is then completed by either the in-house or outside counsel and allows that team to look at the most important documents and issues. The key takeaway: the end result can be a better product at a lesser cost.

For many companies with large volumes of litigation, eDiscovery, document review and technology decisions are a constant priority. In-house attorneys will need to be able to handle eDiscovery and technology decisions, including deciding what portion of the technology process and/or document review should be maintained in-house and what should be outsourced. The options are numerous and vetting technology vendors and review solutions can be costly, challenging and time consuming. Once a selection has been made, in-house attorneys don't get to sit back and relax. Due to the relentless pace of technological change, legal departments are almost constantly forced to review potential new technology solutions; many corporate legal departments, in fact, have a yearly process in place for vetting and selecting new vendor resources. There is currently a growing trend for cloud-based solutions that will continue to alter the face and number of technology vendors in the market. Cloud-based solutions allow businesses and law firms to become more efficient and cost-effective; however, as we discussed in Chapter 2, we can't forget there may be ethical implications for storing and sharing of confidential information outside of your company. For the immediate future, there are still questions being asked within the legal industry regarding privacy concerns and the implications of storing data in the cloud.

As in-house counsel, you'll be faced with many uncertainties that require complex and adaptive decision-making on your part, including needing to make decisions on which "new technology" is best, most appropriate or most cost efficient.

LIFESTYLE LAWYERS THAT ARE MANAGING THE INSOURCING FOR THE CORPORATE LEGAL DEPARTMENT

In addition to using technology solutions, corporate legal departments are trying out new ways to work and save costs by insourcing legal work. The practice of bringing vendors inside to support the legal department has continued to grow, bringing with it new responsibilities for the in-house attorney to manage the growing vendor relationships and creating new delivery models.

> "There are many more participants in the legal ecosystem now than there were several years ago. Outside counsel is only one component."
>
> —Jennifer Williams Alvarez[53]

Many in-house legal teams have turned to vendors as partners for their business's strategic goals and challenges; this can be a

106

win-win for both sides. Hiring experts in a particular service line to support a small (or stretched) legal team can bring a better product to the table and eliminate catastrophic mistakes.

With advances in technology, outside resources can log into legal and business networks and assist with a variety of tasks. A survey conducted by the Association of Corporate Counsel supported the notion that in-house legal departments are bringing outside attorneys into their legal model.[54] The increase in corporate requests to integrate the services of onshore and offshore attorney teams and bring the resources in-house on a project-by-project basis to support the internal team will continue to increase as software and technology solutions improve.

We're now seeing a trend where legal departments are attempting to integrate outside vendor resources into their day-to-day operations, with these vendors providing what I would call "legal business support services."

Setting up a process like this with a large internal attorney team takes patience, time and effort. Without consistent and appro-

> *"Two-thirds of firms report losing business to corporate law department insourcing."*
>
> —*Altman Weil, Inc.*[55]

priate project management, outsourcing or insourcing can just become an expensive add-on that only drains money and time from the legal department. However, with the appropriate project management and the right mix between in-house attorneys, law firms, and vendors, the legal department can create a successful combined business arrangement where everyone works together, as Richard Susskind writes, to "identify ways in which the most straightforward, procedural, and administrative-based activities and tasks can be sourced differently, whether by outsourcing, offshoring, using paralegals, computerizing, or deploying any of the various sourcing strategies."[56] These processes will continue to evolve, especially over the next five to ten years as technology changes bring more innovation. If you're interested in technology and working in-house, there will be opportunities for you to distinguish yourself as the attorney who takes the lead in establishing new technology solutions, ways of working, and managing relationships with vendors—all of which provide the legal department with a more cost-efficient process.

POOLING OF LEGAL SERVICES ACROSS AN INDUSTRY

Another very intriguing model predicted by Richard Susskind in his book *Tomorrow's Lawyers* is based on the idea of pooling legal service providers within an industry. Susskind suggests that similar businesses will begin to figure out how to reuse legal services across the industry in a "collaborative" manner.[57]

In the eDiscovery world of document review this has been happening for several years. Parties on the same side of the "v" will frequently hire a vendor-managed attorney team to review the documents that have been produced in the case. These documents are less sensitive as they're being produced to all parties in the litigation. An outside review team can easily identify important documents and develop a tagging system where parties can benefit from the one-time review of the documents, rather than hiring five separate teams of attorneys to review the documents separately. One could easily see how with forward-thinking attorneys this type of "pooling" or "collaboration" of resources could be extended to other types of legal service deliverables.

There will continue to be a tweaking of the systems as more technology is brought into the legal department to replace manpower (whether that's attorney manpower, paralegal manpower, or vendor manpower). How and when the business processes end up being woven into the legal departments will vary. As in-house counsel, you can expect to increasingly be confronted by these trends and changes to workflow in the legal department. Enabling the process of incorporating the technology with the right vendors and communicating well to get buy-in from your entire organization will help ensure the technology and process moves your solution forward and not backward.

TRUE STORIES OF WOMEN ON THE CORPORATE PATH

One female attorney I interviewed—we'll call her Sandra—has traveled down many different career paths in her 20 years of practicing law. In fact, she's taken at least five of the career paths we'll explore in this book. Since graduating from law school in 1998, Sandra has worked at a small firm in Idaho and a large firm in Oregon; she's been self-employed as a contract attorney, worked in-house for a company in Portland, and she's now working a less traditional job for a large national firm as an associate working remotely, not on a partnership path. Not surprisingly, Sandra talked about how her ambitions during law school failed to line up with her real-world experience as an attorney. It took some creativity and ingenuity on her part to find the legal career with the lifestyle benefits she wanted.

As Sandra progressed in her career and became a mother, she was stressed trying to find the time to do her job and trying to "juggle the family and be present while in either the attorney or mom role." The continued stress at work and her desire to have more balance in her personal life led her to try many different jobs—she was looking for lifestyle benefits long before I came up with the term. When I asked her if there was one job that had been the most fulfilling to her, she stated, "I think I learned the most from being in-house counsel as I had to wear so many hats and be prepared for any type of issue, as well as deal with a very headstrong president of the company." Ultimately, Sandra chose to leave the in-house counsel position and take a less demanding job as an associate working remotely for a large U.S. law firm— she chose the benefits of being a lifestyle lawyer with a hybrid law-firm position. This transition let her fulfill her own personal goals and provided the lifestyle benefits she wanted. It allowed her to continue using her law degree while being able to be at home with her children and play a larger role in their day-to-day lives without giving up her career.

Just like Ruth in Chapter 8, Sandra exhibits a strong sense of needing to work. Her story also reflects the grit it takes to capitalize on the new legal/technology industry to make her career work for her, with lifestyle benefits she needs to be a happy attorney at work and at home.

Unlike Sandra, whose journey to her lifestyle lawyer job took many turns, some attorneys are fortunate to find a more direct route to their ideal job. The highest-paid female General Counsel on the books to date is Denise F. Keane, who retired in 2017 as the General Counsel of Altria Group, Inc., with reported earnings of $9,000,500 in total compensation for her final year in the job.[58] She originally joined Philip Morris USA as an attorney in 1977 and had been in-house with the Altria family of companies for 40 years before her departure.[59] Keane is another example of a female attorney who has been rewarded for her hard work and dedication.

FINANCIAL IMPLICATIONS OF GOING IN-HOUSE

There are some financial advantages and disadvantages when you move to an in-house career. Obviously, the benefits and compensation packages will vary depending on the company's size, market value, and industry. In some instances, larger publicly traded companies will provide information on compensation and benefit packages for the current General Counsel. You may also want to consider working with a staffing agency or online resource to try and determine expected salary ranges for the organization based on your experience. The Robert Half Salary Guide for 2018 reports an average salary range of $128,750 to $306,000 for a General Counsel. In-house counsel with over ten years of experience can expect to make between $114,500 to $255,750. In-house counsel with less than nine years of experience will average between $63,500 to $190,750.[60]

In addition to the amount of your salary, it is important to understand whether the company is willing to provide you with an employment contract and severance package or whether you'll be an "at-will" employee. If you're an "at-will" employee, your job security will depend on your success in your position and the financial success of the company. It may also depend on the leadership of the company. A change in the CEO position, for example, may automatically mean a change in the general counsel position. You can also expect to change jobs more frequently in-house. One report indicated that on average a General Counsel changes roles every 6.67 years.[61]

HOW TO TRANSITION TO THE CORPORATE PATH

If you're interested in the corporate path, carefully consider how you might navigate this transition. Keep in mind the following actions you'll need to take and questions you'll need to answer:

- Are you willing to move? If not, you'll likely be limited to working for in-house companies in your immediate vicinity. For many of us this will dramatically reduce the available employment options.

- When you've identified a position at a particular company that you're interested in:

  - Evaluate the personality and reputation of the CEO and the GC before you accept the position.

  - Evaluate the stability of the company and the industry.

  - Find out how large the in-house legal department is and understand the implications of working in a department of that size.

  - Determine in advance the questions you can ask at an interview to make sure that the company you are working for is on track to be around in five to ten years. They may not be, so you'll also want to ask yourself if you would be willing to take a job with a company that doesn't have a "vision" in the future of the new legal industry.

- Once you land a job in-house, consider joining the Association of Corporate Counsel (ACC).

10

THE SOLO PRACTITIONER & LEGAL CONSULTANT PATH

You would be hard pressed to find an established lawyer that has not considered starting their own business as a consultant or as a solo-practitioner at some point in their career. Honestly, it sounds like an attractive path. You may already feel ready to hang up your shingle or put your new website together and give it a go. But before you do this, you need to understand if this is the right career choice for you.

According to recent statistics available from the National Women's Business Council, between 2002 and 2012, the rate of employment in female-owned businesses grew at a rate of 4.5 times the rate of all businesses and the number of female-owned businesses grew at a rate 2.5 times the national average.[62] While these statistics are exciting, it's important to note that "the report also indicates those businesses still remain significantly smaller than average. Women-owned businesses comprise 36% of the country's businesses, but they employ seven percent of the private-sector workforce, and only contribute four percent of business revenues."[63] I'm citing the overall statistics for women-owned businesses because it was surprisingly difficult to find the statistics for women-owned law practices. The ABA provides yearly reports on women in the practice of law, entitled "A Current Glance at Women in the Law," but there is no category or mention of women that have started practicing law on their own. While it's clear that women are ready, willing, and able to start up their own businesses, it's less clear how many women attorneys are doing so and how successful they are once they've started their own practice.

WHAT TO EXPECT WHEN YOU GO TO WORK FOR YOURSELF

Attorney Scale: 40% to 60% legal focus & 40% to 60% business focus

Pay: The average reported income for solo practitioners has decreased by 16 percent from 2009 to 2011.[64] IRS Income Data for solo practitioners reported an average of $49,130 per year earnings in 2012.[65]

Getting started: It can be argued that opening up your own law office or private practice is the most difficult route that you can take. It'll be helpful if you have prior experience running a business, a specialized practice or area of expertise, and very little competition. While you don't have to land a particular position to get going, you'll need to continually land clients to remain on this path. You may have to work hard to distinguish yourself from others and will have to keep up with the day-to-day logistics of running and owning a business.

Once you have the job: Look for ways to create a marketing solution that'll provide a consistent flow of new clients. Look out for business issues that'll eat up your time and prevent you from bringing in new clients and making money. Learn how to delegate business administration issues to others so you can focus on making money and growing your business.

Lifestyle Benefit – Flexibility: You'll have flexibility to work when you want; you're the boss. But you'll also be working longer hours to bring home a salary and keep the business going. If you think billing two thousand hours a year is difficult, this might not be the best choice for you.

Watch out for: You'll bear all of the responsibilities, including doing work that can't be billed to a client. You'll need to understand and know how to manage and operate the office. You'll need to be watching the money to make sure your business is bringing in more than is going out. You'll be in charge of collections from clients that don't pay their bills. You'll be in charge of marketing. For better and for worse, you'll be in charge of everything.

Lifestyle Benefit – Vision compatibility: This is an excellent career path for attorneys that are entrepreneurial at heart and have the dedication, will and perseverance needed to build their business. If rainmaking is your thing, this could be an excellent career path.

THE FEMALE LAWYER AS A SOLO PRACTITIONER

The 2015 National Association of Women Business Owners (NAWBO) survey reported that the number one reason women said they wanted to start their own business was to own a business and see the business grow; it wasn't for more work-life balance.[66] And that would be expected. Starting your own business is hard work. Being a female solo practitioner can often be the most stressful of the six paths that you can take, yet with all of these challenges, as someone who has recently made the choice to be self-employed, I understand if you still have the desire to go out on your own. I also understand the difficulties involved in taking that first step and committing to starting a new business.

There are certain conditions that might make this path more advantageous for you, or possibly help set you up for success. Here are a few of them:

- You have a large book of clients and a specialized practice that will allow you to open up your own office with immediate work.

- You have a built-in network of attorneys you know in your community that will feed you work that comes into them that isn't the type of work that they do.

- You live in a small town with few attorneys and little competition.

- You have natural business acumen.

- You aren't afraid to take on any type of case to keep work coming in the door.

- Advertising through radio, television, and telephone books doesn't faze you in the least. You're willing to do what it takes to get your name out there and bring in the business.

- You really want to work for yourself. You don't like working for others.

- You're in transition or between jobs for a period of time and you don't want it to look like you're unemployed.

If you see yourself or your situation reflected in one or more of the above statements, this path might already look pretty appealing. But before you start rewriting your future, don't forget that as a solo practitioner, you're not only faced with the daily challenges of practicing law but also the stress and uncertainty of running your own business. There are no guaranteed clients, vacations, benefit packages, maternity leaves—the list goes on.

That being said, this can be a great path. If you have a solid reason for starting your own business and possess healthy amounts of skill, drive, and innovation, the solo-practitioner path can lead to an extremely fulfilling and prosperous career.

HOW TO GET STARTED AS A SOLO PRACTITIONER

Once you have decided to embark on this path, there are several ways to get started. The first way is to literally go out and start from scratch. Open an office and just get the ball rolling. Yet while this may seem reasonable and what many people might imagine starting out to look like, in my more than twenty years of practice I can think of only one or two female attorneys I know personally that have taken this approach. (And I would point out that these women lived in mid-sized cities or small towns. Whether you're male or female, the small-town solo practitioner is still a common choice where job opportunities for lawyers are more limited, the cost of living is less and competition is slim.)

A more preferable way to starting your own firm would be to apply a more transitional approach, where you continue in your current position, if you have one, for a period of time while you prepare to embark on your own. Being a solo practitioner takes planning and time to get your business up and running (which means more capital to get going) and comes with more uncertainty of where and how to land your first clients. Unless you buy or join a small established practice, possibly with a family member or friend (which would likely make getting started much easier), you can't avoid these initial challenges that require extensive planning and preparation.

In a report prepared by the Tennessee Lawyers' Association for Women, the biggest issue of concern for women lawyers in a solo or small practice was networking to bring in business.[67] If you're on your own, you have to be prepared to bring in your own business. Unless you have a constant source for a book of business, you need to be ready to take on any type of case that presents itself. You need to be prepared to advertise everywhere and do whatever it takes to bring in clients. These are important things to consider before you start your own law practice, as many attorneys will not find marketing and rainmaking to be a natural fit for their personality.

Other areas you will need to plan for and address before entering a solo or small firm practice include the management of the office, hiring of staff, marketing and rainmaking, getting your bills paid, staying on top of your own law license requirements, which includes staying up-to-date on the latest developments in the practice of law, and maintaining your own work-life balance at the same time.

TRUE STORIES OF WOMEN ON THE SOLO PRACTITIONER PATH

Every female lawyer I know personally that has become a solo practitioner has a father or mother that had a solo practice. Of course, this isn't a requirement, but it's definitely a factor that may play a part in your decision to open up your own business. Did you grow up with a parent that had a successful solo practice? Odds are if you did and you saw this type of career working, you will have more comfort with it and access to the information needed to start out on your own. You may even be in a situation where you inherit the business.

Another woman lawyer I interviewed, "Sonia," did just that. Her father had been a very successful solo practitioner in their small town; after law school, she got her LLM from Georgetown University and moved to Little Rock, Arkansas, where she practiced at the Attorney General's office. But when it came time to have a family, she had to decide whether to stay in Little Rock in a 9-to-5 job or return to her hometown of Hot Springs to join her father's practice when he retired. After three years of practicing law with the government, she decided to move back to Hot Springs, where she would have the support of her family and friends along with the flexibility of working for herself.

When I interviewed Sonia for this book, she was 20 years into her practice as a solo practitioner. Not surprisingly, she revealed that one of the most challenging aspects of her job as a solo practitioner was bringing in new business. What I didn't expect to hear—having not started on this path yet myself—was that she had experienced a gender bias from clients who wanted a male (or in some instances a female) attorney to handle their case. While some clients would ask for a female lawyer when they called the office, more demanded that a male attorney handle their case. Nothing Sonia can do will change some clients' perception that they're better served by a male attorney. Others have been able to distinguish themselves precisely because they're female attorneys. One notable example is Susan Carns Curtiss, an Oklahoma City litigator who has made a name for herself as the "Girl Attorney." No really she has–in fact she even has a website www.girlattorney. com and has national and individual state Facebook groups for girl attorneys. She often tells the story that when she first started practicing law she would tell new clients that, if they couldn't remember her name when they called the office, to just ask for the "girl attorney."[68]

Even when you are practicing law on your own, you may not be able to get away from gender biases in the courtroom or in your local community. Unfortunately, there is still a public perception that female attorneys practicing on their own are generally divorce attorneys, and while you can work to change this perception, you need to be aware of it and plan for the challenges it may bring to your career.

If you're going to go down the path of a female attorney that is practicing law as a solo-practitioner, or even in a small law office, be mindful of what you do well and the biases that you may face. Exercise your strengths in your practice and look for others to help you fill in the gaps with their unique qualities when needed. If you're the rainmaker, but don't love being in court, make sure that you have a partner in your office to help with the big trials. Look for successful role models that you can emulate to distinguish your legal practice, your firm's image, and guide you in the process.

Another female attorney who has made a name for herself because she's a woman is Gloria Allred. After earning her JD from Loyola University School of Law, where she graduated cum laude, she started her law firm the next year with two male classmates, Michael Maroko and Nathan Goldberg. Her LinkedIn page indicates that the company size is currently between eleven and fifty employees. Allred's list of honors, awards and recognitions in the legal industry is extensive, and includes the President's Award from the National Association of Women Lawyers; the President's Award for Outstanding Volunteerism, which President Reagan presented to her at the White House in 1986; and the Lifetime Achievement Award from The National Trial Lawyers for her groundbreaking work on behalf of women and minorities.[69] Allred is clear proof that a female lawyer can start her own successful law practice and make a name for herself on the national level. Most of us don't know Michael Maroko or Nathan Goldberg's names.

FINANCIAL IMPLICATIONS OF GOING OUT ON YOUR OWN

You have the potential to make more or less money! That is up to you, and depends on what you bring to the table, what you put into your business, and what you aim for. Do you just want to pay the bills and get by or have you decided that is just the beginning? Either way, in most situations, money will be a primary concern as you start your own practice or consulting business.

As you begin to consider the financial implications of this path, consider whether there are multiple streams of income you can tap while you are growing your business. For example, is there a situation where you can still work with your old law firm on a part-time basis while you start your new separate practice? Can you get your license to mediate cases while you build your practice? Or maybe there is a local job outside of the legal field that will give you a source of income, insurance benefits, and potentially access to the public and more clients? Be on the lookout for whatever can provide you with a source of income while you move toward realizing your vision.

HOW TO GET STARTED AS A LIFESTYLE LAWYER CONSULTANT

While not a true solo or small law firm practice, I've included independent legal consulting work in this section because it requires many of the same personality traits and includes similar hurdles in getting started. Like with a solo practice, you'll need to be in charge of your own business from start to finish. You'll eat what you kill!

Consulting is a popular path for lawyers with a little time and experience under their belt. This can be a highly rewarding career financially and in quality of work-life balance. Many lawyers-turned-consultants report that moving to consulting work was a positive step that allowed them to focus on their area of expertise while helping others. Creating your own legal consulting practice will be well suited to attorneys that have a creative personality and are good at building a vison and business strategy. Just as with starting your own law practice, you'll also need to be comfortable selling yourself and your ideas to potential clients. You'll need to be self-motivated, creative, strategic and passionate about your business.

Your first step as a consultant will be to identify, in detail, the type of service and expertise that you'll provide. Spend some real time here outlining what your brand will look like and the unique value and customer benefits that clients will receive from working with you. What are the organizations or other businesses that you'll partner with to make this vision a reality? Who is your competition? You need to know what is going on in your industry and what is making others successful. Keep track of the wins and losses of other similar consultants or businesses and use this for inspiration and learning. This part of the process could take three months or it could take two years; don't rush it. And don't forget that you may need to bring in an expert to assist you and provide structure, support, and clarity. There are an infinite number of steps to lead you toward your new goal and business vision. You're looking for the steps that fit. This is where a trusted resource or career coach may be helpful, to help you be realistic about where you are and what you still need to do to increase your chances for success. A career coach can be indispensable because there can be a very subtle difference between an excellent business plan and a mediocre one.

Once you have your initial core business idea, service line offering, and your vision in writing, you need to start thinking about how you can work toward starting your business and marketing your services. Now you can really get started, set your strategy into play and commit a period of time, at least one year, to devote yourself to this strategy. Make sure that your website and marketing materials are professional and get yourself out in the market. Are you going to market your services to in-house lawyers in legal departments, or will your services be better sold to another entity of the business? As you start your legal consulting practice, remember to keep your eyes open and be responsive to new developments and information you learn as your business knowledge grows.

HOW TO TRANSITION TO THE SOLO PRACTITIONER OR LEGAL CONSULTANT PATH

If you're interested in the solo practitioner path, carefully consider how you might navigate this transition. Keep in mind the following actions you'll need to take and questions you'll need to answer:

- You need to have a plan. You need a plan centered on building your personal brand. This should convey the unique value and benefits clients will receive when they work with you.

- You need a plan centered on strategy and execution. This plan needs to be in writing and it needs to be a living plan that grows as your business develops and changes.

- You need a plan centered on how you'll become successful and who'll help you along the way. What are the products, services, and solutions that you'll be delivering? Are there organizations or other businesses that might partner with you to make this vision a reality? For example, are you going to focus on eDiscovery solutions? If so, what is your target audience? Are you selling to corporations, law firms, or both? Are there technology vendors that you can partner with that will help you sell your services and market you to clients?

- Set your strategy into play and commit a period of time, at least one year, to devote yourself to giving these plans the best chance to succeed.

- Outsource solutions when it's economical and efficient. It'll save you time and money, and you'll end up with a better product.

- As you plan and get started, don't forget that you may need to bring in an expert to assist you and provide structure, support, and clarity. There are an infinite number of steps that can lead you toward your new goal and business vision; a trusted resource or career coach may help you be realistic about where you are and what you still need to do to increase your chances for success.

11

THE ALTERNATIVE LEGAL
SERVICE PROVIDER PATH

In the legal and business worlds the alternative legal services industry has finally caught on and is growing rapidly. The idea of alternative legal service providers (ALSPs) isn't new. What *is* new is the type of legal support we're seeing today. Legal support services are evolving! What we're seeing is a new era of ALSPs offering more specialized, higher-end legal services. Now, in-house legal departments have more options than just keeping work in-house or sending their work to an outside law firm. Demand is growing, and these new companies need lawyers.

The ALSP world can provide excellent employment opportunities for female lawyers—as an attorney working for the company's legal department, a liaison between clients and projects, a sales facilitator, a service line developer, or as upper management leading the company.

An ALSP is basically a company that provides attorneys to assist with the completion of legal services. In some instances the attorneys will complete the entire task; in others they will only provide support for the completion of a legal activity. Most frequently this will be a service for the legal department in a company, but you'll also find instances where these services are performed for other departments in a company and for law firms. Some of the services offered include attorney-managed services, eDiscovery, contract management, patent work, due diligence, regulatory risk and compliance, legal research and legal drafting.

What's fueling the growth in the ALSP industry? Originally, the main attraction for businesses was the cost savings compared to using a traditional law firm. There's now a growing trend for legal ops innovation where corporations are unbundling legal services to design new ways to improve the in-house workflow without adding more people (and, of course, to save money).

The Bloomberg Law 2017 Legal Trends Survey reported that legal procurement will continue to move work to less traditional ALSPs.[70] Yet despite the recent trend to use ALSPs in more facets of the legal industry, many legal procurement professionals don't feel they're actually receiving substantial value from ALSPs, yet.[71] Keep in mind this is a young profession—and the survey also showed that legal procurement professionals plan to keep using ALSPs. According to the report, the industry does believe that working through the process will eventually bring a successful and value-driven relationship that will be positive for the bottom line.[72] Even with the uncertainty regarding their value, ALSPs are still saving companies money. The survey reported a savings of somewhere between 8 percent and 23 percent, depending on the success of the project.[73]

Some ALSPs are also creating subject matter experts. Cost is clearly a driving factor in the use of ALSPs, but over the past decade many ALSPs have also become industry experts, specializing in a particular legal area along with the technology used to support deliverables in their field. As technology solutions have become more sophisticated and complicated, the expertise of those working in the ALSPs industry has become increasingly specialized and nuanced. Corporate buyers are looking for this specialized knowledge that will provide a cost and time savings as well as the best final product. This is where the ALSP industry is headed.

And what does that mean for you?

Well, if you're motivated to learn how to work with new business delivery models or use the most advanced technology solutions on the market today, this can really be a place to distinguish yourself. You may need to think about your career slightly differently than before; you may even have to take a pay cut at the start. But aligning yourself in a position where you are set to learn the best practices and the best technology solutions in a particular area of legal operations support can really give you the potential for a long-term career trajectory. Don't think short-term here—think about building a unique skill set that can eventually lead to more job security, higher wages, specialized skills or more job flexibility.

WHAT TO EXPECT WHEN YOU GO TO WORK FOR AN ALSP

Attorney Scale: This will vary dramatically with the type of position you take. You can find positions working 100% as an attorney for an ALSP, but in other instances the range of legal work is much more limited: 5% to 30% legal focus, 50% business focus and 20–25% other.

Pay: Since this is a new industry, there's not yet a set pattern or expectation regarding pay. For example, you can work as a contract attorney doing document review work in Florida and receive as little as $30 per hour, or you can work for a rising new Legal Process Outsourcing (LPO) company on the sales team and make more than $500,000 a year. But on average, you can expect to make less in this industry than you would at a traditional top-tier law firm.

Getting started: Many of these jobs provide repetitive, lower-end solutions, so they're not sought out as much as other jobs with wider scopes. This opens up the field and makes it generally easier to get started on this path.

Once you have the job: Look out for pigeonholing yourself into a small sliver of legal services delivery; always keep your eyes open for ways to build your résumé and your expertise within the industry.

Lifestyle Benefit – Flexibility: The beauty of the ALSP industry is that the jobs typically come with a significant level of flexibility. Almost all jobs in this industry will be lifestyle lawyer jobs. You can potentially negotiate for the benefits or working options that offer you the lifestyle you want.

Watch out for: Signs that the company isn't succeeding. ALSPs are new players in a new industry, and many won't make it. With this in mind, realize your job may not be around this time next year.

Lifestyle Benefit – Vision compatibility: This is an excellent career path for attorneys interested in blazing a new trail, looking to bridge a gap between careers, or looking for more flexible work environments.

WHAT CAN TAKING A POSITION AS A LIFESTYLE LAWYER WITH AN ALSP MEAN FOR YOUR CAREER?

We continue to see companies entering the legal market that are built on the idea of providing the best packaged solutions to businesses looking to navigate the growing complexities and choices of the "new law" market in a particular practice area or niche market. To be successful, these companies need lawyers to sell, provide and deliver the services. You'll see new roles for lawyers as salespeople, educators/trainers, project managers and relationship managers for these "new legal" business solutions. You may see one legal specialist whose only function is to be a liaison between the client and the judge or court, another trained and equipped to interact with judges or testify on how the computer or software works or verify that the machine has done its job correctly. The list of possible jobs for attorneys in this industry will continue to grow.

At these new legal services companies, you'll find jobs available for senior legal talent with prior work experience at big law firms and in corporate legal departments, along with jobs for attorneys fresh out of law school. The variety and number of new jobs ALSPs create translates into more opportunities than ever to have a law career that meets and expands your skill sets and supports your lifestyle choices. Attorneys in the ALSP industry have a good chance of achieving a work-life balance.

Another advantage of working for an ALSP is the ability to make connections with attorneys in the legal departments of some of the world's top corporations and law firms. It's therefore an excellent way to open doors and build connections that might lead to your next job. Young associates at law firms will generally not get these types of introductions and interactions with clients. Paired with the right ALSP, you might end up getting more experience and networking opportunities than you ever dreamed possible.

For all the opportunities that ALSPs offer, remember that unless you are on the sales team, these jobs are not likely to be the highest-paying with the best benefits. This may seem like a clear disadvantage to the career path, yet it comes with a platform to negotiate for what's important to you and your career. Perhaps you want to gain certain experience, or you want to work from home or part-time. If these are your priorities, the reality is that you may have to accept fewer benefits, less security or less pay. In satisfying your deepest priorities, though, you often gain much more than what a generous compensation package can offer. Whether or not this is the right path for you simply depends on your mindset and your vision for yourself. And in the end, you may end up with a special set of skills and connections that distinguishes you in a way that does command the big paycheck or job security in a way that you didn't anticipate when you started down this road.

Let's take a look at some of the ALSPs that currently provide legal jobs for attorneys who want the benefits of a less traditional job.

LEGAL PROCESS OUTSOURCING (LPOS): ONSHORE AND OFFSHORE

In the early 2000s we started to see companies offering legal process outsourcing services for the U.S. legal market. The first LPOs were eDiscovery shops offering large-scale document review services.

At the outset, two types of LPOs existed: those based in the U.S. ("onshore" LPOs) and those based overseas ("offshore" LPOs). The onshore LPO shops were originally started by large U.S. law firms that set up separate document review teams with contract attorneys and sold these services—at a lesser rate but a high-profit margin—to their clients. These onshore document review facilities were extremely profitable for law firms. We also started to see companies not associated with a law firm set up onshore attorney teams to do document review work. Generally these teams would be based in low-cost markets in the U.S.

Offshore LPOs based in low-cost countries such as India or the Philippines also started to come into the marketplace; these offshore companies were a natural growth from the successful introduction and expansion of the business process outsourcing (BPO) industry. Today, it's not uncommon for ALSPs to offer both onshore and offshore legal solutions, along with other services such as technology solutions.

As the legal market changed and technology advanced, these outsourcing businesses have expanded service-line offerings from document review to also include contract management, legal research, due diligence, patent work and more. Large U.S.–based companies functioning as legal-outsourcing service providers now have a wide array of offerings: litigation services, law department consulting, contracting solutions, intellectual property, cyber-risk solutions and others. An interesting result of this highly specialized industry has been the creation of a lower-cost "super expert" or "lifestyle-lawyer expert." This is partly due to the amount of time that these attorneys (whether onshore or offshore) have spent on repetitive tasks on a variety of technology platforms. Many clients rightly see these attorneys as leaders in understanding how to use technology in a particular area of the legal delivery process. These are attorneys who play a crucial role in providing the best value and defensible product to their clients.

At the outset, businesses typically engage LPOs on a project-by-project basis to work at an hourly rate or for a flat fee. Additional alternative pricing options may also be available depending on the relationship with the client, the size of the project, the current workload at the LPO, the project type and other factors. I've recently started to see businesses purchasing per-seat attorney positions with LPOs. Jobs with these companies include full-time and part-time positions, as well as contract work.

Some of the larger LPOs you may want to consider working for are Thompson Reuters (Pangea3), UnitedLex, QuisLex, Integreon and CPA Global. If you're interested in a position with one of these companies (or with one of the many other LPOs), it would a good idea to develop some technology and business skills to couple with your law degree. Many certifications on the market can be instrumental in landing a position with one of the bigger companies.

ALTERNATIVE LEGAL SERVICES COMPANIES

More and more companies are adopting alternative ways to provide legal solutions. They give businesses the ability to hire traditional attorneys to perform legal work on a contract, fixed project or temporary basis. Whether you think of these businesses as a new type of law firm or a service provider that facilitates linking businesses with contract lawyers, they're gaining recognition and a portion of the legal market.

These companies offer flexible positions for the lawyer: they provide a variety of jobs with different terms of commitment. You might have the luxury of choosing your assignments based on your immediate needs and availability. You can gain experience by landing a job with a new corporate client. And long-term commitments with companies may ultimately lead to a full-time position.

Offerings of these new legal service providers range from the traditional attorney services to less-traditional consulting roles: helping businesses improve strategy, develop legal operation solutions and implement process improvement and technology solutions. These companies typically hire attorneys with a variety of traditional specialties: banking and finance, commercial contracts, employment law, intellectual property, and regulatory and compliance. They also hire them to perform more standardized work like including managed review, contract management and discovery. These companies will maintain large rosters of lawyers and then pair an appropriate attorney with the business or law firm that needs help. Think of them as providing temporary staffing solutions. Current leaders in this industry are Axiom Legal, Counsel on Call and Elevate Services.

LIFESTYLE LAWYER POSITIONS IN PROJECT MANAGEMENT AND MANAGED SERVICES

With the introduction of new business models into the legal arena, we're seeing the need for attorneys with a specialized knowledge of project management and legal departments to serve as liaisons between attorneys, IT personnel, vendors and litigation support professionals to make sure that services are delivered as promised.

To meet this need, ALSPs introduced attorney-managed services and service management consultants (SMCs). The goal is to develop overall strategies to move businesses into forward-thinking service delivery models that bring multiple entities together to meet specific client demands. The SMCs provide companies and law firms with end-to-end solutions (sometimes bringing together multiple entities) for a specific problem or service delivery. These consultants offer a deep understanding of available technology solutions, the ability to provide large-scale manpower on long- or short-term projects, industry-specific expertise and an understanding of the company's business needs.

The SMC will oversee vendors' work, whether they be technology providers or LPOs (onshore and offshore). An attorney in this role will generally be a more senior U.S. attorney or an experienced subject matter expert with a strong T-shaped background that helps her lead the project, drive the numbers, and keep staffing and delivery on track. This position is crucial when dealing with an offshore team of attorneys with different levels of experience, varying expectations of timelines for delivery, and who work in different time zones. SMCs may end up taking a permanent position within a company or continue to work as consultants on best methods for managing legal projects, compliance outsourcing and other specialties.

The legal project manager will often be tasked with vetting providers and making sure the work product is up to expectations, on time and within budget. She'll bridge the gap between the in-house litigation team, outside counsel, and one or more vendors on a given project.

Legal project manager positions might include the following titles:

Practice Support Project Manager: This is frequently a consultant position with a vendor; it requires knowledge to support technical and litigation questions throughout the EDRM.

Senior Project Manager: Senior project managers are expected to have a strong understanding of Relativity and other eDiscovery software solutions. Relativity certification is an asset in job searches and salary discussions.

Litigation Support Case Manager: This is a hybrid role which often requires advanced technology skills, including familiarity with document review platforms and eDiscovery workflows. The ideal candidate has a JD and experience working on varied eDiscovery software solutions.

Client Support Manager: This role will frequently require advanced technology skills across several different types of software solutions, including Contract Lifecycle Management software, eDiscovery software, artificial intelligence software solutions and others. The ideal candidate has a JD and experience working on varied software solutions across multiple industries. Depending on the size of the company they may even be tasked with onboarding or vetting new technology solutions for clients.

Senior Litigation Support Analyst: This position is responsible for processing data and supporting a litigation case team, serving as an interface between attorneys, paralegals and vendors. Experience in multiple review platforms is a plus.

LIFESTYLE LAWYER POSITIONS WITH ONLINE LEGAL SOLUTION SERVICES

ALSPs also include a growing number of online legal service providers. These online providers are already in the legal marketplace—think RocketLawyer, LegalZoom and Wevorce, just to name a few. We can expect to see continued growth—potentially an explosion—of online legal solutions as the public becomes more comfortable with the idea, and as more lawyers and clients enter the legal revolution. This will mean new opportunities for lawyers as corporate counsel for the business, as staff attorneys to support the business teams, and as sales support. We'll see increased opportunities in this industry in the coming five to ten years. If you're interested in this field, consider joining a local technology group to learn more about up-and-coming startups in your area.

TRUE STORIES OF WOMEN ON THE ALSP PATH

Many of the female attorneys I interviewed and work with are either already on a less-traditional legal path or want to transition to one. Working for an ALSP is clearly an avenue to make this happen. For the female attorney looking for a flexible schedule, a truly remote job, a way to make more money, or a way to inhabit both the legal and business worlds at the same time, this could be an ideal path.

One female attorney I spoke with—we will call her "Elena"—had worked over ten years at one law firm without being on the partnership track. She'd even left to work for judges two different times, then returned to the firm, but intentionally chose not to be on the partnership track. Still, she felt pressure to conform to the standard law firm expectations; although the partners had agreed to let her work part-time, Elena felt some of them didn't entirely approve of her part-time status. When given the opportunity to work for an ALSP, working remotely as an independent contractor, she leaped at the chance. In her new position, Elena no longer has to deal with feeling that her work/life choices are not accepted by her employers. She has autonomy over her day and how much work she does. While she's generally happy with the change, she says she feels "challenged by the loss of a steady income and the financial benefits of being employed by a large firm."

Part of the process of being a lifestyle lawyer is realizing what's most important to you in your legal practice. Sometimes this means you have to make *hard* choices: you may have to forego a big salary and some job security in order to have that "perfect job."

One woman who's a visionary in the Alternative Legal Services Industry is Jane H. Allen, the founder of Counsel on Call in Nashville, Tennessee. She received her JD from the University of Kentucky and practiced law with two regional firms before founding Counsel on Call in 2000. At that time, the ALSP industry in the U.S. had barely begun. Jane truly had insight and a calling when she set out to change the legal market.

When Allen started her business, her goal was to combine the practice of law with business needs to provide quality, cost-effective legal solutions.[74] She absolutely did it!

She also wanted to provide a way for attorneys to do what they enjoy, in a manageable atmosphere, while making a positive difference.[75] She did that too!

Today, Allen is a recognized industry expert and speaker on a variety of legal and business issues, and her company has been named one of the 500 fastest-growing privately held companies in the U.S.[76] Oh–and she recently started making handbags with her sister; you can see her handiwork at www.hannerclarke.com. This is a woman in charge of her life!

FINANCIAL IMPLICATIONS OF WORKING WITH AN ALSP

Pay will vary significantly from company to company and job to job in this industry. Obviously, if you're signing up as a contract attorney, you'll need to be aware that your paycheck may not be consistent: you'll be employed when there's a need. Be prepared for that range in compensation and look for a job that best fits your experience and situation. It will be the lifestyle benefits of most jobs with ALSPs that make this an attractive alternative for many female lawyers.

HOW TO TRANSITION TO THE ALSP PATH

If you're interested in the ALSP path, carefully consider how you might navigate this transition. Keep in mind the following actions you'll need to take and questions you'll need to answer:

- Are you using this job to land your next one? One advantage of working for an ALSP is the potential for making connections with attorneys in the legal departments of the world's top corporations and law firms. With this in mind, try to position yourself as advantageously as possible by finding an ALSP with clients you want to connect with.

- When considering a particular ALSP to work with, think through the following:

  - What's the company's global footprint? If you're interested in working abroad, this could be a stepping stone to making that dream a reality.

- Do you have any ethical concerns with the company's services or what they're asking you to do as an attorney—especially if it's a newer, cutting-edge group?

- What's the stability of the company?

- Do they provide error and omissions or malpractice insurance?

- Do they allow you to work remotely?

12

EDISCOVERY PATH

Evolving technology has created a new specialty for attorneys in the field of eDiscovery. In the prior chapters, we touched on eDiscovery. Yet because the field of eDiscovery continues to be one of the fastest-growing markets in the legal industry, it truly warrants its own chapter. Let's take a deeper dive into the field of eDiscovery and the potential jobs for female attorneys in this burgeoning industry.

First, why is the industry growing? Despite efforts to control discovery costs, including the 2015 revised Federal Rules of Civil Procedure, the cost of discovery is still a significant factor associated with taking a case to trial, and as data volumes grow exponentially, the cost and management of eDiscovery has continued to be of great importance to businesses and the legal industry as a whole. On average, companies report spending $3.5 million dollars on eDiscovery services for a medium to large-sized case—these figures include both attorney time for reviewing documents and the cost for technology services.[77] There is no end in sight as data volumes and new sources of electronically stored information increase.

However, there have been significant advancements in the eDiscovery platforms used to review documents. Attorneys are able to use cluster visualization, technology assisted review, deduplication and many other tools to make the review process more manageable and expeditious. Continued technological advancements will benefit U.S. attorneys in this industry, allowing them greater access to the data they need to represent their clients, increasing the ability to pinpoint needed information to win cases, and helping control the cost of discovery. Some attorneys see developing technology as a threat; they argue the technology will advance to the point that attorneys are no longer needed and review work will be fully assumed by robot attorneys and artificial intelligence. While I do believe we will continue to see advancements in eDiscovery review capabilities, I don't believe attorneys will be eliminated from the review equation. For the foreseeable future, we will continue to see numerous jobs for trained attorneys with eDiscovery experience.

WHAT TO EXPECT WHEN YOU GO TO WORK IN THE EDISCOVERY INDUSTRY

Attorney Scale: 25% to 30% legal focus & 50% business focus & 20% to 25% other

Pay: In some markets you will find U.S.–barred attorneys making as little as $20 per hour to $40 per hour.[78] I've seen salaries for project managers or leads ranging from between $80,000 to $110,000. TRU Staffing Partners reported that in 2016 and 2017 the average base salary for a new Electronical Stored Information (ESI) sales position was between $175,000 to $195,000.[79]

Getting started: There are many large law firms and eDiscovery vendors that'll have entry level positions for eDiscovery attorneys to do document review work. These jobs will likely be by the project and won't pay well, unless you bring an additional skill to the table like a foreign language. Having a Relativity software certification or a certification from another technology solution that's in high demand will help ensure that you have fairly consistent work and can make you marketable for a full-time or management position in the field.

Once you have the job: Once you've learned how to use the technology solutions, the actual document review work won't usually be difficult and you should be able to leave it at the office. Continue your education and stay up-to-date on the most recent developments in technology. This will keep you at the top of the game.

Lifestyle Benefit – Flexibility: This will depend on how you plug yourself into the eDiscovery world. If you're doing actual review work as a contract attorney, you'll likely have the flexibility to pick which project you work on. It's important to note, though, that once you're working on a project you may have to work extended hours to meet delivery deadlines.

Watch out for: Being categorized as "just an eDiscovery attorney." If you still dream of being the lead attorney on a big trial one day, you should know that by taking an eDiscovery job you might be taking yourself off that career path, unless you're using the position as a means to get yourself to the next level. Be careful of staying in an eDiscovery position for too long, if this is not your end goal.

Lifestyle Benefit – Vision compatibility: This is an excellent career path for attorneys interested in technology. If you want to make more money in the eDiscovery industry, become an expert in the technology supporting it.

WHAT IS THE STATE OF THE EDISCOVERY INDUSTRY TODAY?

The eDiscovery document review industry is changing each day with the introduction of new technology solutions and mergers of key eDiscovery and technology companies. Looking not too far ahead there are three key things that I see happening in the next five to ten years with eDiscovery technology and document review services.

First, technology prices as a whole have been and will likely continue decreasing. Technology tools that were difficult to afford just seven or eight years ago are now available at comparably reasonable costs. Second, attorneys will increasingly have access to high-end technology tools. The introduction of document review platforms on a cloud-based system, high-end document review services, including TAR, AI, and ECA (early case assessment) advanced analytics, are becoming less expensive and more accessible to all attorneys, not just those at big law firms with deep pockets. Third, skilled eDiscovery attorneys will be able to control, to some degree, the volume of documents being reviewed by attorneys.

The increased accessibility to the latest and best eDiscovery solutions will allow fewer attorneys to handle larger volumes of data. This, in and of itself, will be a good thing in the effort to keep costs in control. Skilled attorneys that are proficient in using advanced eDiscovery tools will have the upper hand at pretrial conferences and settlement negotiations. The side with the most technology-savvy attorney— who knows what technology tools are available, how to use the tools, and how to bring the narrative together to give an accurate assessment of client data—will be best positioned to paint a complete story early on in the case and articulate a convincing position to a judge. Attorneys will be able to control what data is accessed and reviewed in the case and use this information to limit discovery to a more manageable data set. In the end, eDiscovery specialists will get better results for their clients with less cost and manpower.

Although larger cases will still benefit from outsourcing a portion of the eDiscovery process to onshore or offshore attorney teams, skilled eDiscovery attorneys will increasingly control the amount of work being outsourced as they are able to get an early handle on the data and limit the number of documents that are required to be reviewed.

Subject matter experts in eDiscovery will be in demand in other ways as well. We will continue to see more social media, audio, video, and other non-text data files as part of production requests, and this will raise new questions: What technologies will be available to review these nontraditional forms of data? How will this data be reviewed? How will you be able to incorporate the review of this nontraditional data into your workflow? These new considerations will open up doors for the technology-savvy attorney, presenting them with opportunities to prosecute and defend cases involving eDiscovery negligence, act as an expert witness for eDiscovery cases, or consult on the electronic discovery reference model (EDRM) process from start to finish.

ETHICAL RESPONSIBILITIES LAWYERS OWE THEIR CLIENTS REGARDING EDISCOVERY?

As we discussed in Chapter 2, lawyers must possess a certain level of proficiency to represent a client and handle their case, and today, this duty of competency also includes a requirement that a lawyer is abreast of the risks and benefits of relevant technology, while continuing to maintain confidential and privileged client information.[80]

The Wells Fargo data breach in the summer of 2017 highlighted the potential pitfalls of having an attorney handling an eDiscovery production without having the necessary technical knowledge or training on the software used in eDiscovery projects. "Unbeknownst to me, the view I was using to conduct the review has a set limit of documents that it showed at one time," said the Wells Fargo attorney, a New York-based principal at a respected law firm, in her affidavit. "I thought I was reviewing a complete set, when in fact, I only reviewed the first thousand documents."[81] The result of this "inadvertent misunderstanding," as she called it, was that she turned over customer information including personally identifiable information without a confidentiality provision or redactions being applied.

Without a technology-savvy attorney, a specialized expert vendor, or a validation process in place, the potential damages from malpractice claims will continue to rise as data volumes increase and technology advances.

WHERE DO WE SEE EDISCOVERY HEADED?

In *The Third Wave: An Entrepreneur's Vision of the Future,* Steve Case writes that "the Internet of Things sensor and tracking technology will give companies unprecedented access to an extraordinary level of detail about our everyday lives: not just what food you purchase but your eating habits; not just how much energy you use but how cold you like it when you sleep at night."[82] Privacy questions as well as security implications will be at the forefront of these new issues.

We're seeing new laws in response to privacy and security considerations as technology changes and grows at unprecedented rates. In the U.S. the field of privacy and data protection has skyrocketed in the past 20 years. Protecting personally identifiable information will only continue to grow as new technology drives constant change and impacts new sectors with each new invention. Each month we see reports of new and bigger data breaches.

The European Union has responded with the GDPR, the most recent comprehensive data protection law to attempt to standardize privacy and protection across the EU states. The law mandates new and enhanced obligations with more stringent protection of personal data rights, and expands the concept of personal data and the protections afforded to the individual, through among other things, a "right to be forgotten" provision, the ability to award significant fines for noncompliance, and a requirement that companies appoint a data protection officer.

EU authorities are concerned there is a lack of harmonization and an unbalanced use of personal data over the internet. The goal of the GDPR is to try and provide a more coherent data protection plan with stronger enforcement that allows further development of the digital economy and brings about legal and practical certainty.

Implementing a data classification plan to organize data and putting a retention and preservation plan in place is a critical practice for organizations in order to save and secure information. When a litigation or potential litigation arrives, this will allow corporations to know where its data is and how to put a litigation hold in place on this data. The more data, the more information is available—but there are costs associated with accessing this data. This is a fairly new industry so the technology solutions to handle the collection and the review of Internet of Things (IoT) devices are just starting to take off and their current costs may be prohibitively expensive in some instances. One would expect that for the near future, attorneys will be successful in making proportionality arguments pursuant to FRCP 26 (b) (1) that the cost and burden for producing IoT data is prohibitively expensive. But as technology advances and prices come down, courts will start allowing more parties access to relevant information found in IoT data.

Increasing volumes of data, evolving technology, and recent judicial sanctions have created a need for eDiscovery privacy specialists. If you're considering entering this field, you'll find attorneys working under a variety of titles, including eDiscovery document reviewer, eDiscovery specialist, eDiscovery project manager, eDiscovery advisor, eDiscovery consultant, and others. You'll find these jobs with law firms, ALSPs, corporations, and government agencies. Your job will include not only completing the work, but educating the client on the complexities of eDiscovery, the legal technology needed, and the process required to ensure compliance with new rules and regulations while completing discovery in the most defensible and value-driven method.

TRUE STORIES OF WOMEN ON THE EDISCOVERY PATH

This is one area in the practice of law where you may find women in the majority of positions. Some of the female attorneys I've worked with have intentionally focused on distancing themselves from the eDiscovery component of their practice, while others have used it as a career builder.

Defining what success looks like means identifying what's important to you. But just as in all walks of life, if you do things well, with pride, and passion, you're very likely to rise to the top. While some attorneys find eDiscovery to be a "lesser" field of the law, others have identified themselves with eDiscovery and used their expertise and specialty in this fast-evolving area to distinguish themselves. In my case, I took my second career path as an eDiscovery attorney (though how and to what extent this will play into my third career path is still on the table). I now regularly speak at events on eDiscovery, legal operations and technology. I'm eagerly looking forward to the changes that the legal industry and eDiscovery will see in coming years. I'm a female lifestyle lawyer with no regrets—working for an ALSP allowed me to work remotely when my kids were young and be a part of an evolving business/legal market that has opened up even more career opportunities for me.

Another female attorney who has embraced the new legal world and created her own career in eDiscovery is Kelly Twigger. A graduate of Marquette University Law School, she worked as a partner in a law firm for 12 years leading the firm's commercial litigation and eDiscovery practice before she started her own firm, ESI Attorneys LLC, in 2009. ESI is a unique firm with a sole focus on helping law firms, corporations and government entities with eDiscovery and information law.[83] Her firm provides assistance and processes to handle eDiscovery and technology solutions. Along with founding ESI, Twigger is also the creator of eDiscovery Assistant, a web-based company that gives lawyers the information and tools they need to keep up with electronic discovery.[84] Specifically, they provide access to eDiscovery case law, eDiscovery specific rules, eDiscovery forms and checklists. Twigger has found unique ways to repackage and deliver top-of-the-line eDiscovery solutions outside of a traditional law firm format.

FINANCIAL IMPLICATIONS OF WORKING IN EDISCOVERY

Pay will vary significantly from company to company and job to job. As stated previously, if you're signing up as a contract attorney you'll need to be aware that your paycheck may not be consistent; you'll be employed when there are projects that require your services. In the eDiscovery industry there is generally an ebb and flow of work that is completely unpredictable, so if you're looking for a consistent paycheck this may not be the best choice for you. Another factor to consider is that U.S. contract attorneys in the eDiscovery industry have seen a significant dip in their hourly rate. In some markets you will find U.S.–barred attorneys making as little as $20 per hour (in the Dallas market) to $40 per hour (in the California market).[85]

This isn't to say that all jobs in this industry will require you to take a substantial cut in pay. Sales executives in the eDiscovery industry can be very well paid for their successful book of business. TRU Staffing reported that in 2016 and 2017 the average base salary for a new ESI sales position was between $175,000 to $195,000.[86] Note this is the base salary; with good sales and commissions you can be looking at well over $500,000 for the year. I've included two of the extremes, but the truth is you'll find these scenarios and everything in between when you enter this job market. Be prepared for the variance in compensation and look for the best fit for your experience and situation.

HOW TO TRANSITION TO THE EDISCOVERY PATH

If you're interested in the eDiscovery path, carefully consider how you might navigate this transition. Keep in mind the following actions you'll need to take and questions you'll need to answer:

- If you're in a large firm, first consider volunteering to work on an eDiscovery project before you commit to this path fully.

- If you're looking to obtain work as a review attorney on an eDiscovery review project, substantive litigation experience in a law firm or corporate environment and a working knowledge of the EDRM lifecycle will give you the upper hand when you apply for jobs. Experience working on multiple eDiscovery platforms and the ability to perform advanced searches with eDiscovery platforms will also set you apart.

- Obtain platform training or certification in Relativity, iCONECT by Xera, Catalyst, or others.

- Obtain certification with nationally recognized programs such as the Association of Certified eDiscovery Specialist (ACEDS).

- Become an active member of The Sedona Conference or the Electronic Discovery Institute (EDI), consider EDI's Mentorship Program, and join Women in eDiscovery (WiE). Make use of free resources from The Sedona Conference, such as The Sedona Principles, Third Edition.[87] These organizations and resources will keep you up-to-date on the most recent trends in the eDiscovery industry.

- If you want to make big money, you may want to eventually end up in sales. Start building your skill set in this area now so that when the opportunity presents itself, you're a strong candidate.

13

CYBERSECURITY & PRIVACY PATH

One of the newest career paths for lawyers is in the cybersecurity and privacy field. With potential damages from a cyberattack being in the millions of dollars, this market is set to explode; in fact, the global cybersecurity market is expected to exceed $202 billion by 2021.[88] Reports project cybercrime damages in excess of $6 trillion by 2021, with a cybersecurity expert shortage of over one million jobs.[89] According to CyberSeek, in 2017 the U.S. employed 780,000 people in cybersecurity positions with approximately 350,000 cybersecurity openings.[90] Lawyers with a privacy background and/or technology expertise are in high demand to help businesses and law firms with compliance and risk, incident response plans and privacy issues.

If this is an area that interests you, take some time to get up-to-date on the state of the cybersecurity and privacy industry and consider whether this path makes sense with your current work experience and education. Then consider what, if any, additional training you can obtain to help you land your desired job in this fast-growing field.

WHAT TO EXPECT WHEN YOU GO TO WORK IN THE CYBERSECURITY INDUSTRY

Attorney Scale: Chief information security officers (CISO) = 10% to 50% legal focus & 50% technology focus; chief privacy officer (CPO) = 80% legal focus & 20% technology focus

Pay: Unlike the eDiscovery market, which has been maturing for the past decade, the cybersecurity privacy market is relatively new. Due to the lack of qualified professionals in the cybersecurity/privacy arena, salaries are relatively high and should stay that way for the foreseeable future. The IAPP reported in its yearly salary survey that the average salary for a lawyer working as a privacy professional in 2017 was $141,600.[91]

Getting started: These positions may require additional education or certification to land a job. Consider a Certified Information Security Manager (CISM) or Certified Information Privacy Professional (CIPP) certification. While not everyone in this industry is an attorney, don't let this fool you, this is not an easy test. The IAPP reported that most privacy professionals came to the privacy field with a legal background and prior career as an attorney.[92]

Once you have the job: If you're working for a vendor, remember the market is still developing; you can expect to see changes and acquisitions in the years to come. Always be prepared and keep certifications and résumés fresh and relevant.

Lifestyle Benefits: These positions have the potential for flexibility, depending on what part of the industry you choose to work.

Watch out for: The inability to stop all cyberattacks. As hackers become more advanced and our information becomes more digitized, it is harder to prevent cyberattacks. With this in mind, you'll need to be prepared to deal with the fallout from a breach. This may not be the job for you if you're looking for a low-stress position that you can leave at the office.

Vision compatibility: This is an excellent career path for attorneys interested in privacy, technology, and getting started down a new career path in a relatively new industry. If you're up for more learning and complex challenges, this field is ripe with opportunities for lawyers like you.

WHAT IS THE STATE OF THE CYBERSECURITY AND PRIVACY INDUSTRY TODAY?

The internet has brought great changes to our world and created a globalized way of working; in fact, many of the jobs and topics discussed in this book depend of the interconnectedness made possible by the internet. However, along with the numerous benefits, this interconnectedness has also created a culture of cybercrime. Today, everyone—individuals, companies, law firms—is at risk from the threat of a cyberattack of one kind or another.

A security breach can come from inside or outside of an organization, and can be either unintentional or malicious.[93] The potential for business operational risk, reputational risk, and legal and compliance risk is the damage that an organization might face from a cybersecurity incident.[94] According to a report from Northcentral University, all businesses large and small are at risk, but the damage from just one breach can be devastating to a small business. "43 percent of cyberattacks target small business, and 60 percent of small companies go out of business within six months of a cyberattack."[95] The stakes are already high, and as businesses continue to become more digitized and use IT to optimize business processes, the risk from a cyber threat will only continue to grow.

So one of the goals of cyber-risk management is to control the damages. Experts identify cyber threats and design risk mitigation and response plans to limit the damage done in an attack. To protect an organization, one needs to look at technical issues and human risk factors. It may surprise you to learn that most of the successful cybersecurity incidents involve human error. In short, cyberattacks are frequently caused by simple things people do which expose private information, data, and computer systems: many breaches are the result of systems not having passwords, systems having obvious passwords ("password1"), or the act of clicking on a phishing email.

One of the more popular and successful means of attack comes from phishing email scams, which are becoming increasingly sophisticated and harder to detect. One such phishing scam put a Los Angeles defense firm in the spotlight in the summer of 2017. The firm was involved in a settlement that required an initial payment of $500,000 to the settlement administrator.[96] Online scammers managed to intercept and respond to several emails and over time were able to issue an email to the defense firm that appeared to be from the administrator of the settlement fund and contained fraudulent wiring instructions.[97] The defense firm, not knowing this was a phishing scam, unknowingly forwarded the email to the defendant, who subsequently paid the $500,000 into the inaccurate account.[98] This wasn't the first time attorneys have fallen for a phishing scam and it won't be the last. Another similar phishing attack involved the payment of $63,000 that was earmarked for settlement.[99] In this case, an email that appeared to be from the plaintiff's attorney instructed the defense counsel to wire the remaining $63,000 in settlement payments to a specific bank account.[100] In this unique case, the plaintiff's attorney was held responsible for the loss of the missing funds as they had knowledge before the transaction that a hacker was targeting the funds, but failed to inform defense counsel of this threat.[101] In both cases, a simple phone call or two could have prevented the criminals from walking away with the money.

The damages from cyberattacks will continue to grow. Cyberspace has united our emergency preparedness communications, critical digital and process control systems, and infrastructures. The protection of these systems is so essential to our economic and national security that the Department of Homeland Security's (DHS) has created a resource for shared situational awareness of malicious cyber activity. DHS's National Cybersecurity and Communications Integration Center (NCCIC) is a 24/7 cyber situational awareness, incident response, and management center.[102]

Growing threats are setting the stage: more cyber experts and privacy professionals are needed to help implement processes and protect organizations and customer data from cybercrimes. In addition to these experts representing and advising clients on cybersecurity issues, they'll also be needed internally to help law firms develop their own cybersecurity plans. According to the 2016 ABA Legal Technology Survey Report, 62.8 percent of law firms with 500 lawyers or more reported that potential clients demanded that law firms meet security requirements and have a detailed cybersecurity plan in place.[103] With cybersecurity requirements and demands continuing to increase, it will remain an important industry to follow even if you're not planning to move into cybersecurity or privacy as a specialty.

ETHICAL RESPONSIBILITIES LAWYERS OWE THEIR CLIENTS REGARDING CYBERSECURITY?

In 2017, we saw an increase in document leaks, data breaches, and virus attacks to the point where you can't turn on the television, open your phone, or look online without hearing or reading about the topic.

In response, the American Bar Association (ABA) provided new guidance in 2017 to ensure attorneys have an understanding of some basic steps that should be considered when dealing with the ever-changing arena of technology and the well-established requirement to protect client information and communications. On May 17, 2017, the ABA's Standing Committee on Ethics and Professional Responsibility issued Formal Opinion 477. In the opinion, the committee acknowledged that the basic obligation of an attorney to maintain confidentiality has not changed. However, the "role and risks of technology in the practice of law" has changed.[104] This opinion is an update to ABA Formal Opinion 99-413, issued eighteen years ago in 1999, and it's intended to provide additional assistance and guidance to attorneys on how to protect client information and communications.

Opinion 477 points out the use of technology and email communications by attorneys has grown exponentially since the 1999 opinion. Attorneys and their staff "now regularly use a variety of devices to create, transmit and store confidential communications, including desktop, laptop and notebook computers, tablet devices, smartphones, and cloud resources and storage locations. Each device and each storage location offer an opportunity for the inadvertent or unauthorized disclosure of information relating to the representation, and thus implicate a lawyer's ethical duties."[105] But when using the internet and technology, an attorney may be required to "take special security precautions to protect against the inadvertent or unauthorized disclosure of client information."[106]

Sadly, this guidance has come a little late for some attorneys and their clients. In *Harleysville Insurance v. Holding Funeral Home,* a senior investigator uploaded video surveillance of the fire loss scene and the entire investigation file onto an Internet-based electronic file-sharing service. He then sent an email with a hyperlink that was not password protected. The link was shared with defendant's counsel—and all the unprotected information (including the case investigation file containing privileged information) was hosted and available without any password protection. Given the lack of restrictions to access the site and the absence of basic document-level protections, the magistrate judge found that the attorney-client privilege had been waived by the client's conduct. The opinion states: "In essence, Harleysville has conceded that its actions were the cyber-world equivalent of leaving its claims file on a bench in the public square and telling its counsel where they could find it."[107] Judge Sargent went on to state, "the technology involved in information sharing is rapidly evolving. Whether a company chooses to use a new technology is a decision within that company's control. If it chooses to use a new technology, however, it should be responsible for ensuring that its employees and agents understand how the technology works and, more importantly, whether the technology allows unwanted access by others to its confidential information."[108]

On appeal, the district judge found that the disclosure of privileged information was inadvertent and that privilege was not waived.[109] However, the magistrate judge's words regarding a company's responsibility to ensure that employees understand new technology should not be overlooked. At best, this was a six figure mistake and the message remains the same. As an attorney you need to know how to use technology to keep your client's confidential and privileged information secure.

As we've discussed, companies are exploring the landscape of service providers, service models, and platform choices, and analyzing the risks and benefits that different models offer. For corporations struggling with oversight, accountability, and efficiency, technology savvy privacy attorneys will be valuable to analyze processes and make hard choices.

BUILDING YOUR CYBERSECURITY AND PRIVACY EDUCATION

Cybersecurity and privacy issues will only increase as new technologies are developed. As we briefly discussed in the last chapter, emerging issues will be plentiful as Big Data and the Internet of Things (IoT) are the next big trends in technology.

In the last several decades, there has been a rapid increase in the types of technology being developed and the data that is being collected. Smartphones are just one of the new technologies that have resulted in an increase of Big Data that can track the most intimate details from our daily lives. There is almost no end to what is being captured by our phones, who we are speaking to, who we've spoken to, where we are throughout the day, what is the current state of our health, where we are in our home, you name it!

Where does all of this Big Data go? What is being done with your personal data? Analysis of this data brings potential for benefits and risks. As we all know, one breach of a centralized database can result in a costly loss of personally identifiable information.

Since damage to an organization's IT networks can result in financial and reputational damage and litigation risk, executives need to thoroughly understand and make wise decisions regarding cybersecurity risk. As businesses look for support in this critical area, there will be a growing demand for attorneys that understand cybersecurity, privacy and the regulatory landscape; can explain the issues, risks, and available options to executives and board members; and can help them manage these risks.

In order to transition successfully to the cybersecurity industry, you don't need to be able to program and write code, but you do need to have some knowledge of how systems and networks work. What if you don't have this background and you need to start from scratch? I recommend doing an online course or certification course that'll give you a working knowledge of cybersecurity issues, including cyber threats and cyber-risk management. Ideally, this course would also give you an understanding of the IT environment, including the hardware, software, and networks that are at risk and need to be protected. This isn't required, but it's a good idea to have a solid understanding of the IT environment to couple with your legal education.

Another way to enter the cybersecurity world is by building up your privacy knowledge and experience. One route is to obtain the Certified Information Privacy Professional/U.S. certification or European Union certification (CIPP/US or CIPP/E), both are offered by the International Association of Privacy Professionals (IAPP). The CIPP/US and CIPP/E certifications are designed to demonstrate that you have obtained a comprehensive understanding of U.S. or EU privacy laws and regulations and that you also understand how to responsibly transfer and handle sensitive personal data.[110] If you choose to pursue either of these, I would advise you to dedicate an appropriate amount of time to study for the exam. You can expect it to be challenging. Trust me on this one—I know from experience!

The "constant change in information technology means constant change in the challenges facing privacy professionals. . . . Privacy professionals are at the forefront of crucial changes in society."[111]

WHAT YOUR WORK IN THIS WORLD MAY LOOK LIKE

If you enter the cybersecurity and privacy world, you'll be constantly thinking through how legal, IT and compliance teams can work together to protect data. The first step will be to get a better understanding of what data exists within the business and where it is being stored. As cyberattacks become increasingly harder to stop, containment of a data breach becomes more important than ever before. If you don't know what data you have and where it is being kept it will be harder to protect.

Next, you'll need to consider whether you can have one unified storage location that provides a single point of access to the protected class of data (such as personally identifiable information). One location can help you simplify what you need to protect, monitor when a breach occurs, and control and contain the damage once an intruder is inside your isolated network.

Additionally, you may frequently be tasked to set up processes to respond to and control better business initiatives to govern the corporation's data. This will help to strengthen your internal cybersecurity and compliance. The process of setting up workflows that drive internal processes to make decisions regarding data is complex, but can bring a significant return on investment if done correctly.

Through all of this, you will help train your team. Remember that people are the number one cause of data breaches, so employees must be trained to deal with technology and follow established workflows to properly handle and protect technology. Systems need to be tested and audited on a regular basis.

CYBERSECURITY AND PRIVACY POSITIONS FOR ATTORNEYS

Chief information security officer (CISO): These experts are predominately tasked with setting information security policy and strategy. They also ensure a business is compliant with cybersecurity regulations and client requirements.

155

Chief privacy officer (CPO): Generally, a CPO will work to ensure ongoing activities within an organization are consistent with privacy policies on a federal and state level. The CPO will also be instrumental in responding to client audits and specific client requests that pertain to cybersecurity/risk.

Data protection officer (DPO): A DPO is a security position that is required by Article 30 of the Global Data Protection Regulation (GDPR). This position is responsible for ensuring there is a sound strategy in place to protect data and that a company is compliant with GDPR requirements. The DPO position is new to many companies and is still evolving. At this time, there is no requirement that the DPO position be filled by someone with a law degree; there is, however, a requirement that the DPO have a strong understanding of the technical components of the job. It'll be interesting to see this position develop further and see whether any educational or certification requirements will be required to ensure certain capabilities or expertise.

TRUE STORIES OF WOMEN ON THE CYBERSECURITY AND PRIVACY PATH

Although cybersecurity centers on technology, an industry predominantly controlled by men, there are some female lawyers leading the way in this challenging, rapidly changing field. One notable female attorney is Julie Brill. Brill received her law degree from New York University School of Law. After serving as the Assistant Attorney General for Consumer Protection and Antitrust for the State of Vermont, she was appointed by President Obama in 2010 to serve as Commissioner on the Federal Trade Commission, where she received wide acclaim and was "seen as the commission's most important voice on Internet privacy and data security issues."[112] She held this role for six years before becoming partner and Co-Director of Privacy and Cybersecurity at Hogan Lovells. In April 2017, Microsoft announced it had created a new role for Brill, overseeing privacy and regulatory affairs.[113]

According to Microsoft's press release, she will "lead privacy, data protection and other regulatory issues as head of its Privacy and Regulatory Affairs Group. . . . Brill's new role will extend beyond privacy to include areas such as telecommunications regulation, corporate standards, internet governance, as well as legal and regulatory issues around accessibility of Microsoft products."[114] Brill is certainly making her mark on this emerging field.

I can also give you a first-hand account of a female attorney considering the cybersecurity path. I recently completed an online course at HarvardX in cybersecurity; as I'm finishing *Lifestyle Lawyer* I have studied for and passed the CIPP/US exam. In addition, I'm attending technology conferences and speaking with government officials to try and determine whether the legal side of this industry will be a good fit for my personality, skill sets, education and life goals. I've taken a considerable amount of time over the past six months to look at potential jobs for attorneys in cybersecurity. As I do so, I'm looking at successful women like Julie Brill to inspire and stretch my goals in this industry. At the same time, as I said earlier, there's an inherent risk in this field: while most of us won't make the national press while engaged in the practice of law, in the cybersecurity industry we're opening ourselves up to national notoriety if a breach occurs while we're in charge. In my case, I'm still evaluating whether the lifestyle benefits in cybersecurity are worth the potential cost.

FINANCIAL IMPLICATIONS OF WORKING IN CYBERSECURITY AND PRIVACY

In the cybersecurity and privacy path, you have a lot of options because you can work as a consultant for law firms, corporations, government entities, and vendors. Additionally, this is a relatively new industry where you have more flexibility to design your own career. With high demand and a large number of open positions, wages for qualified professionals are likely to remain fairly high for the foreseeable future. Reported salaries for chief information security officers (CISOs) range from between $186,872 to $246,907 as reported by salary.com on November 28, 2017.[115] The IAPP reported in its yearly salary survey that the average salary for a lawyer working as a privacy professional in 2017 was $141,600.[116] Privacy professionals (note these will not all have law degrees) with an IAPP CIPP/US certification reported a median salary of $151,064 in 2017.[117] The highest reported salaries were found for chief privacy officers (CPOs) in the U.S., with an average base salary of $191,000.[118] Lawyers working in the U.S. for large law firms in the banking or software industry also reported the highest salaries.[119] Other factors such as working for the government, working for small companies or firms, or working in small cities can significantly impact the expected compensation packages.[120]

HOW TO TRANSITION TO THE CYBERSECURITY AND PRIVACY PATH

If you're interested in the cybersecurity and privacy path, carefully consider how you might navigate this transition. Keep in mind the following potential options to beef up your credentials:

- Take a class. Lawyers can take cybersecurity or privacy courses through many different organizations, many of which offer online education. One example is the online course I took through HarvardX.

- Get certification. If you're looking at potential jobs and employers are recommending or asking for certain certifications, those are the certifications that matter. Consider a Certified Information Privacy Professional (CIPP) certification—either the U.S. or the EU. You might also take a look at the Certified Information Privacy Manager certification—it revolves around day-to-day privacy operations and processes.

- Get real-world experience. Develop an internal cybersecurity threat analysis for a client or your company.

- Get set up with a solid set of news sources to keep you up-to-date in the cybersecurity world.

- Consider starting a website or a blog as a place to share your contact information, a list of your accomplishments or services, and well-written, informative posts that discuss the latest cybersecurity developments from a lawyer's perspective. You might also consider building your reputation as a cybersecurity expert by providing regular LinkedIn or Twitter content.

- Find a mentor with experience and connections in the industry.

CONCLUSION

BE A UNIQUE, HAPPY AND SUCCESSFUL LIFESTYLE ATTORNEY

In the practice of law you'll inevitably come across successful attorneys who look like they really know what they're doing—as if they've always done everything right and were rewarded with this perfect career. It may seem natural that they hold that prestigious position. And then you'll meet someone else—someone who on the surface appears to be remarkably less perfect—but they also appear to have figured it all out. You'll find yourself wondering how they got to that same place. The point is, you can't see behind the scenes to the complicated reality of everyone's path. There are many ways to get where you want, and some of these routes may seem less obvious than others. What's most important is to follow your gut instinct, staying open to every possibility as you identify and pursue your goal. Surrender yourself fully, with faith in your skills and instincts. Hold nothing back and live in the moment. This is the essence of being a lifestyle lawyer.

> *"If you believe in yourself and have dedication and pride—and never quit, you'll be a winner. The price of victory is high but so are the rewards."*
>
> —*Paul Bryant*

I hope you'll find this book helpful as you make decisions on where you want to go in your legal career and how you want to get there. I know that at times the process will be difficult—at least, it has been for me. But I also know this: if you're confident in yourself and your skills, and you set out each day with creativity and ingenuity to achieve something, you'll succeed in ways you never thought imaginable.

I urge you to invest time thinking through what you want, then remain dedicated to your new career plan and path. Always trust yourself, your voice and your ability to reach your goals. That's how you'll get to your destination.

You'll certainly meet people along the way who have chosen a different path. Respect their choices while remembering not to let anyone else dictate yours; use your vision to stay on track. It may take longer than you planned—it might even look different than you expected—but that's okay.

Building a business or changing careers isn't always easy. In fact, it's rarely easy. But you have to stick to your plan. Be persistent!

Fear, distractions and uncertainty will likely challenge you along the way. This may be especially true at the start, when your goals and destinations are far from being realized. When this happens, use this book, your vision and whatever resources available to stay the course and remain centered. When daily life gets in the way or obstacles arise that you can't predict or control, take a breath, go for a walk or run, and challenge yourself to control your response to what's happening. Go for your own unique personal journey and know that, however complicated, it's the right journey. Sometimes you'll just need to let go, surrender and listen to your gut. Realize when you need to move beyond distractions and focus on what's truly important: your end goal and vision in life.

While you must generally persist, persist, persist—there are some things you can quit as you explore different legal career paths:

First, quit second-guessing yourself. If you put careful thought and reflection into developing your plan, believe in it! Improve it and make adjustments when needed, but remember that you created this plan because it gave you the most realistic chance to get what you want out of your life.

Second, quit rushing to your destination. Expect that obstacles and adjustments will slow you down at times. But keep yourself moving in the right direction and just keep going . . . and going . . . and going. Enjoy the process and try to be fully present for the journey.

And third, quit pushing at life. Embrace the opportunities in front of you in this life. Let life pull you! The hard part won't be finding options: the hard part will be weeding through the surplus of offerings, then finding what you believe will move your career forward and complete your vision.

We all have a unique contribution to make to the world. You've taken the time to figure out how to best use your legal talents and make the most of your life. You've taken the time to articulate a vision. Hold on to these things!

Try to think of your end goal at the start of each day. Keep this as your anchor, your focus; don't let yourself get bogged down in minutiae. People generally spend excessive amounts of time arguing and fretting over issues that in hindsight are not important—trust me, I know! For many years I was an expert in this field. Choose to instead center yourself daily in your vision. This will have a profound effect on the way you interact with people and how they see you. When you ignore the little things in life, people—including yourself—will realize that YOU are the boss of your emotions, your actions and your life.

At the end of the day, your plans and choices as you design your legal career are part of something much bigger: you and your life. I don't need to remind you that they affect every aspect of your life. But I might need to remind you how important it is to enjoy the process. Find work that you enjoy and learn from it, make your work part of you and grow with it.

As you grow, I hope you choose to live the life that makes you happy, allows you to take control, and lets you make the most of each situation. You'll benefit not only yourself, but also the people you love—and in some ways the whole world. You've worked very hard to get where you are in your life—be proud of it!

RESOURCES

Here are some of the resources that I use on a regular basis. I hope that you will find these helpful.

My Business Sites
www.lifestyleforlawyers.com
www.lawyersandyoga.com
www.leeholcombconsult.com

Other Helpful Sites
www.thesedonaconference.org
www.ediscoveryinstitute.org
www.iapp.org
www.aceds.org
www.girlattorney.com
www.faughnanonethics.com

ACKNOWLEDGMENTS

After completing my book, which was not a 30-day process, but a year-long process that required several revisions and edits, I'm excited and a little sad to be wrapping up this part of my book project that has been an almost daily part of my life.

I'm extremely grateful to all the people who helped me along the way and gave me the fuel I needed to keep writing this book and moving forward.

To my mother and Ms. Holcomb, who both passed on their unique qualities that have guided me on this life journey.

To my favorite lawyers and neighbors: Howard Vogel, Bruce Fox and Bill Young, who each lent me their ear, expertise, guidance and connections. I couldn't have been more fortunate than to have you all as neighbors and mentors. I will always be grateful.

To the ever-generous and patient Honorable Tim Conner. Thank you for the many, many hours you patiently advised and trained me on not only how to practice law, but when to let things go. I'm sorry you had to hear me ask the same questions over and over.

I also want to thank Jody Burkeen who inadvertently played a part in planting the seed to write this book.

To Leitner, Williams, Dooley & Napolitan, PLLC and Doug Dooley, thanks for giving me my first job as an attorney. What a great place to start my legal career.

To Cobra Legal Solutions, LLC and the entire Cobra Board, for having the vision to build the company and for giving me the opportunity to be part of the new legal world. Thank you all for your time, encouragement and support. I'd especially like to thank Lalitha Janarthanan, Nirmal Nithyanandh and Theophilus Rajiah for their friendship and guidance during my time at Cobra.

To all the people who've been generous in their love, support, time and guidance during this book-writing process, in particular John McMillen, Jackson Webb and Vincent Webb.

To my writing friends (Stacy Ennis and Robin Bethel) who helped me throughout the book writing process—especially Cristen Iris who gave me several hard messages that I needed to hear.

To all of my friends who helped me along the way in this book and in my career. I would especially like to thank Karen Crutchfield, Tonya Wheat Willis, Sherri McDonough, Heather Anderson, Jen Giuttari, Amy Dodds, Samantha Miller and Barbara Squires. Your generous support and kind words have been much appreciated.

To Ann Goldstine and Mary Warren Sanders, thank you for being my friends and my people I come home to.

And special thanks to Nancy Buffington for getting me!

NOTES

Introduction

1. Dubhe Carreno, "This Quiet Dust," Ceramics Monthly, (October 2017), 42.

Chapter 2

2. "Rise of the Rest," accessed September 11, 2017, https://www.riseof rest.com/.

3. Jessica Guynn and Jon Swartz, "Steve Case: 'Third Wave' of Internet Will Help Middle America Business," *USA Today*, June 29, 2017, https://www. usatoday.com/story/tech/news/2017/06/29/steve-case-third-wave-internet-hel p-middle-america-business/102554688/.

4. Rule 1.1, "Duty of Competence," *ABA Model Rules of Professional Conduct*.

5. Ambrogi, Robert, "31 States Have Adopted Ethical Duty of Technology Competence," Updated March 15, 2018,

https://www.lawsitesblog.com/2015/03/11-states-have-adopted-ethical-duty-of-technology-competence.html.

6. Christian Mammen, Jason Lohr, and Hogan Lovells, "The Ethics of Artificial Intelligence in Law Practice," *Law Technology News*, February 8, 2017.

7. Ricci Dipshan, "Federal Judges Say Attorneys' Lack of E-discovery Acumen Still Plagues Federal Courts," Legaltech News, January 30, 2017.

8. Ibid.

9. Mammen, Lohr, and Lovells, "The Ethics of Artificial Intelligence in Law Practice."

10. Ibid.

11. Ibid.

Chapter 3

12. Gary Keller and Jay Papasan, *The ONE Thing: The Surprisingly Simple Truth Behind Extraordinary Results* (Austin, TX: Bard Press, 2012), 55.

Chapter 4

13. Paul Arden, *It's Not How Good You Are, It's How Good You Want to Be* (London: Phaidon Press Limited, 2015), Introduction.

14. Frank Sesno, *Ask More: The Power of Questions to Open Doors, Uncover Solutions, and Spark Change* (AMACO, 2017), 111.

15. https://www.americanbar.org/groups/women/initiatives_awards/ grit.html

Chapter 6

16. Mister Rogers' Neighborhood: Thoughts For All Ages, https://en.wik-iquote.org/wiki/Fred_Rogers

17. R. Amani Smathers, "The 21st-Century T-Shaped Lawyer," *Law Practice Magazine* 40, no. 4, (July/August 2014), https://www.americanbar.org/publications/law_practice_magazine/2014/july-august/the-21st-century-t-shaped-lawyer.html.

18. Ibid.

19. Ibid.

20. "Resources for Lawyers Going Overseas," US Department of State Family Liaison Office, accessed September 9, 2017, https://www.state.gov/documents/organization/253915.pdf.

21. Ibid.

22. Alan Feuer, "A Judge Wants a Bigger Role for Female Lawyers. So He Made a Rule." *The New York Times,* August 23, 2017, https://www.nytimes.com/2017/08/23/nyregion/a-judge-wants-a-bigger-role-for-female-lawyers-so-he-made-a-rule.html?mwrsm=Email.

23. Ibid.

24. "The 2017 Working Mother 50 Best Law Firms for Women," *Working Mother,* July 25, 2017, accessed September 9, 2017, http://www.workingmother.com/best-law-firms-for-women-2017.

25. National Asian Pacific American Bar Association page, accessed September 10, 2017, http://www.napaba.org/.

26. Patricia A. Meagher, "The Women-Owned Small Business Federal Contract Program: Ten Years in the Making," *American Bar Association* 46, no. 2 (Winter 2011).

27. Meagher, "The Women-Owned Small Business Federal Contract Program: Ten Years in the Making."

28. Office of the Federal Register, *Code of Federal Regulations,* 13 CFR § 127.200-202.

29. Office of the Federal Register, *Code of Federal Regulations,* 13 CFR § 127.202.

30. "Women Owned Businesses," US Small Business Administration, https://www.sba.gov/business-guide/grow/women-owned-businesses-programs.

Chapter 7

31. Arden, *It's Not How Good You Are, It's How Good You Want to Be*, 66-67.

32. Laura Sabattini, "Unwritten Rules: What You Don't Know Can Hurt Your Career," *Catalyst,* June 2008.

33. Arden, *It's Not How Good You Are, It's How Good You Want to Be, 30.*

34. Erik Deckers and Kyle Lacy, *Branding Yourself: How to Use Social Media to Invent or Reinvent Yourself* (Pearson Education, Inc., 2013), 30-31.

35. Deckers and Lacy, *Branding Yourself: How to Use Social Media to Invent or Reinvent Yourself,* 7.

Chapter 8

36. "2016 ABA-Approved Law School Graduate Employment Data," American Bar Association, https://www.americanbar.org/content/dam/aba/administrative/legal_education_and_admissions_to_the_bar/statistics/2016_law_graduate_employment_data.authcheckdam.pdf.

37. Ibid.

38. Robert Half Legal, *2017 Salary Guide for the Legal Profession*, https://www.roberthalf.com/sites/default/files/Media_Root/images/rhl-pdfs/2017_salary_guide_roberthalflegal.pdf.

39. Georgetown Law and Thomson Reuters Legal Executive Institute, *2017 Report on the State of the Legal Market* (2017), 1, https://static.legal-solutions.thomsonreuters.com/static/pdf/peer-monitor/S042201-Final.pdf.

40. "2017 Law Firms in Transition: An Altman Weil Flash Survey," accessed September 4, 2017, http://www.altmanweil.com/LFiT2017/.

41. Zach Warren, "Inside DLA Piper's Client Retention Data Analytics Program," *Law.com,* last modified Aug 17, 2017, https://www.law.com/sites/almstaff/2017/08/17/inside-dla-pipers-client-retention-data-analytics-program/?slreturn=20180119225427.

42. "A Current Glance at Women in the Law January 2017," American Bar Association, https://www.americanbar.org/content/dam/aba/marketing/women/current_glance_statistics_january2017.authcheckdam.pdf.

43. "Company Overview of UnitedHealth Group Incorporated," Bloomberg, https://www.bloomberg.com/research/stocks/private/person.asp?personId=32508685&privcapId=10467

44. Rebekah Mintzer, "Here Are the Ten Highest Paid Female GCs in the U.S.," *Corporate Counsel,* December 22, 2017, https://www.law.com/corpcounsel/sites/corpcounsel/2017/12/05/here-are-the-ten-highest-paid-female-gcs-in-the-u-s/.

Chapter 9

45. "Inhouse Counsel Salaries–2018 Guide," *Inhouseblog*, https://www.inhouseblog.com/inhouse-counsel-salaries-guide/.

46. Aebra Coe, "Corporate Counsel Are Keen on Moving Work In-House," April 3, 2018, https://www.law360.com/articles/1029224.

47. Stephanie Forshee, "Legal Departments Want to Add More In-House Lawyers, But Will They?," April 3, 2018.

https://www.law.com/2018/04/03/legal-departments-want-to-add-more-in-house-lawyers-but-will-they/?et=&bu=&cn=&src=&pt=.

48. Ibid.

49. Ibid.

50. Prashant Dubey and Eva Kripalani, *The Generalist Counsel,* (New York: Oxford University Press, 2013).

51. Brad Harris, "Zapproved's 2017 Legal Hold and Data Preservation Benchmark Report," July 2017, 4, https://www.zapproved.com/get-2017-legal-hold-data-preservation-benchmark-report/.

52. Ed Silverstein, "Law Firms, Legal Departments Predicted to Focus More on IT Risk," *LegalTech News*, August 21, 2017.

53. Jennifer Williams-Alvarez, "CLOC Survey Shows Legal Departments Still Spending More Externally," *Corporate Counsel,* November 16, 2017.

54. Brad Harris, "Zapproved's 2017 Strategic eDiscovery Insights and Best Practices," (July 2017), 51, https://www3.zapproved.com/WP_2017_LHDP_PREX16_Proceedings_Full.html?ls=Pay-per-click&ccn=Google%20

Adwords&cid=701G0000000CD6U&_bt=176428514568&_bk=zapproved. com&_bm=b&gclid=Cj0KCQjw3MPNBRDjARIsAOYU6x-Xulafdxz8pfJ1 VL5dtr5QPAzgZneKa1CpkkJTLKrKUc9Teo74tP8aAvl1EALw_wcB.

55. Altman Weil, Inc., *2017 Law Firms in Transition: An Altman Weil Flash Survey*, accessed September 4, 2017, http://www.altmanweil.com/LFiT2017/.

56. Richard Susskind, *Tomorrow's Lawyers: An Introduction to Your Future, Second Edition* (Oxford Press, 2017), 89.

57. Susskind, *Tomorrow's Lawyers,* 89.

58. Mintzer, "Here Are the Ten Highest Paid Female GCs in the US."

59. "Stocks," *Bloomberg,* https://www.bloomberg.com/research/stocks/people/person.asp?personId=43212720&privcapId=296308.

60. "Inhouse Counsel Salaries–2018 Guide," *Inhouseblog.*

61. Dubey and Kripalani, *The Generalist Counsel,* 36.

Chapter 10

62. Jessie Reape, "National Women's Business Council Report Shows Women-Owned Businesses Thriving, Growing," *National Women's Business Council,* news release, March 7, 2016, https://www.nwbc.gov/news/national-women%E2%80%99s-business-council-report-shows-women-owned-businesses-thriving-growing.

63. Ibid.

64. Benjamin H. Barton, *Glass Half Full: The Decline and Rebirth of the Legal Profession* (Oxford: Oxford University Press, 2015), 5-6.

65. Ibid.

66. Steve Strauss, "Hillary, the Glass Ceiling, and Small Business," *USA Today,* August 6, 2016.

67. Tennessee Bar Association Special Committee on the "Glass Ceiling Initiative," *Beyond the Glass Ceiling: Advancing and Retaining Women* (Tennessee Bar Association, 2012), https://tlaw22.wildapricot.org/resources/Documents/TBA%20Glass%20Ceiling%20Report%202012.pdf.

68. "#68: Cultivating Community with the Founder of Girl Attorney," Heather Hubbard podcast, May 1, 2018, http://www.heatherjoyhubbard.com/podcast/cultivating-community-with-the-founder-of-girl-attorney/

69. "About Gloria," Gloria Allred, https://www.gloriaallred.com/About-Ms-Allred/.

Chapter 11

70. Bloomberg Law, *2017 Legal Procurement Survey,* (2017), 7, https://www.bna.com/2017-legal-procurement-m57982084612/.

71. Bloomberg Law, *2017 Legal Procurement Survey,* 9.

72. Ibid.

73. Bloomberg Law, *2017 Legal Procurement Survey,* 11-13.

74. "Counsel on Call–The Practice of Law Reimagined," YouTube video, 5:30, posted by "Counsel on Call," April 15, 2014, https://www.youtube.com/watch?v=dVHQWkQCa3o.

75. Ibid.

76. "Jane H. Allen," Counsel on Call, https://counseloncall.com/bios/jane-h-allen/.

Chapter 12

77. "Electronic Discovery: A View from the Front Lines," Institute for the Advancement of the American Legal System, 2008, 25, http://iaals.du.edu/sites/default/files/documents/publications/ediscovery_view_front_lines2007.pdf.

78. Alex Rich, "So How Much Do Contract Attorneys Really Make?," *Above the Law,* http://abovethelaw.com/2013/10/so-how-much-are-contractors-really-making-out-there/.

79. Jared Coseglia, "The Great ESI Sales Exodus," Law Technology Today, October 25, 2017, http://www.lawtechnologytoday.org/2017/10/great-esi-sales-exodus/.

80. Rule 1.1, "Duty of Competence,"; Rule 1.6, "Duty of Confidentiality," *ABA Model Rules of Professional Conduct.*

81. Christine Simmons, "Lawyer's 'Inadvertent' E-Discovery Failures Led to Wells Fargo Data Breach," *New York Law Journal,* July 27, 2017.

82. Steve Case, *The Third Wave: An Entrepreneur's Vision of the Future* (Simon & Schuster, 2016), 151.

83. "ESI Attorneys – Our History," ESI Attorneys, http://esiattorneys.com/about-esi-attorneys/history/.

84. "Features," EDiscovery Assistant, https://www.ediscoveryassistant.com/features/.

85. Alex Rich, "So How Much Do Contract Attorneys Really Make?"

86. Jared Coseglia, "The Great ESI Sales Exodus."

87. The Sedona Conference, *The Sedona Principles, Third Edition: Best Practices, Recommendations & Principles for Addressing Electronic Document Production* (2017).

Chapter 13

88. Julie Sobowale, "Law Firms Must Manage Cybersecurity Risks," *Crain's Chicago Business,* March 1, 2017.

89. "The Growing Importance of Cybersecurity to Business*,*" *Northcentral University* (blog), May 27, 2017, https://www.ncu.edu/blog/growing-importance-cybersecurity-business.

90. "Cyberseek Supply/Demand Heat Map," *CyberSeek,* accessed September 2, 2017, http://cyberseek.org/heatmap.html.

91. The International Association of Privacy Professionals, *2017 IAPP Privacy Professionals Salary Survey–Executive Summary*, accessed on January 1, 2018, https://iapp.org/resources/article/2017-iapp-privacy-professionals-salary-survey-executive-summary/.

92. Ibid.

93. RSA Security LLC, *Cyber Risk Appetite: Defining and Understanding Risk in the Modern Enterprise* (August 7, 2017), https://www.rsa.com/en-us/resources/cyber-risk-appetite-defining-and- understanding-risk-in-the-modern-enterprise.

94. RSA Security LLC, *Cyber Risk Appetite: Defining and Understanding Risk in the Modern Enterprise.*

95. "The Growing Importance of Cybersecurity to Business*,*" *Northcentral University* (blog).

96. Bonnie Eslinger, "Law Firm Duped by Email Scammers in Wage and Hour Case," *Law 360,* August 23, 2017, https://www.law360.com/articles/957163/law-firm-duped-by-email-scammers-in-wage-and-hour-case.

97. Ibid.

98. Ibid.

99. Ibid.

100. Ibid.

101. Ibid.

102. "Information Sharing," Department of Homeland Security, accessed September 2, 2017, https://www.dhs.gov/topic/cybersecurity-information-sharing.

103. Julie Sobowale, "Law Firms Must Manage Cybersecurity Risks."

104. "ABA Formal Opinion 477," American Bar Association Standing Committee on Ethics and Professional Responsibility, May 11, 2017, https://www.americanbar.org/content/dam/aba/images/abanews/FormalOpinion477.pdf.

105. Jill D. Rhodes and Vincent I. Polley, *The ABA Cybersecurity Handbook: A Resource for Attorneys, Law Firms, and Business Professionals* (American Bar Association, 2013), 3, quoted in "ABA Formal Opinion 477," American Bar

Association Standing Committee on Ethics and Professional Responsibility, May 11, 2017, https://www.americanbar.org/content/dam/aba/images/abanews/FormalOpinion477.pdf.

106. "ABA Formal Opinion 477," American Bar Association Standing Committee on Ethics and Professional Responsibility, May 11, 2017, https://www.americanbar.org/content/dam/aba/images/abanews/FormalOpinion477.pdf.

107. Harleysville Ins. Co. v. Holding Funeral Home, Inc., No. 1:15cv00057 (W.D. Va. February 9, 2017).

108. Ibid.

109. Harleysville Ins. Co. v. Holding Funeral Home, Inc., No. 1:15cv00057 (W.D. Va. October 2, 2017)

110. "CIPP/US Certification," The International Association of Privacy Professionals, https://iapp.org/certify/cippus/.

111. Peter Swire and DeBrae Kennedy-Mayo, *U.S. Private-Sector Privacy, Law and Practice for Information Privacy Professionals, Second Edition*, (International Association of Privacy Professionals (IAPP), 2018), 359.

112. Mike Swift, "Profile FTC's Bill Emerges as Key Player in National, International Regulation," MLex Market Insight, June 10, 2014, https://www.ftc.gov/system/files/documents/public_statements/316381/140610internationalregulation.pdf.

113. Gabe Friedman, "Microsoft Creates New Privacy Lawyer Role," *Big Law Business*, April 28, 2017, https://biglawbusiness.com/microsoft-creates-new-privacy-lawyer-role/.

114. "Microsoft Appoints Globally Respected Regulator to Privacy Leadership Role," *Microsoft Corporate Blogs*, April 28, 2017, https://blogs.microsoft.com/on-the-issues/2017/04/28/microsoft-appoints-globally-respected-regulator-privacy-leadership-role/.

115. "Chief Information Security Officer Salaries," Salary.com, https://www1.salary.com/Chief-Information-Security-Officer-salary.html.

116. The International Association of Privacy Professionals, *2017 IAPP Privacy Professionals Salary Survey–Executive Summary*.

117. Ibid.

118. Ibid.

119. Ibid.

120. Ibid.

ABOUT THE AUTHOR

Photo credit: Dina Curtis

Lee Holcomb started her legal career in 1998 in Tennessee. In 2006, she made partner—and had her first child. When her husband took an overseas position with the U.S. State Department, Lee was at first reluctant to leave her firm. But her desire to have a second child led her to take a giant step. On December 23, 2006, with two small children, she boarded a plane to Poland.

Shortly after she arrived in Warsaw, Lee began planning her return to the legal workforce. This would ultimately take her to India, where she essentially started over in a part-time position with an international legal outsourcing provider. Thus began her second legal career path, which would eventually lead her to become the Chief Operating Officer and Director of Legal Services of the same company.

Lee is currently embarking on the third stage of her career: as an author, speaker, consultant and yoga/wellness coach for stressed-out attorneys.

Made in the USA
Middletown, DE
17 November 2018